Self-Publishing

How to Become a Six Figure Self-Publishing Entrepreneur

Kasim K.M.

Table of Contents

Introduction

The benefits of the digital platform have enabled common people to achieve their dreams like never before. The fact that things are much more accessible to each individual is so impressive.

This could never have been possible without the world of internet, affiliate marketing, e-commerce platforms, and social media networks. One can use such resources for creating a robust online business that promises a consistent passive income for a lifetime.

However, the problem is — *How to do it? Which is the correct way to go about achievingyour dreams in the online world?*

That is where the online prodigy Kasim Mohammed comes in to assist you.

Kasim "Kasguru" Mohammad

For many years, Kasim has established his presence in the online world of self-publishing and other online and offline businesses. Due to his formidable tactics, he is often referred to as Kasguru for his intense coaching and training programs that teach ambitious individuals like you how to reinforce your presence in the digital world.

Kasim is himself a serial entrepreneur, author, affiliate marketer, and a six-figure self-publisher, who has successfully set up several offline and online businesses around the globe. Besides these multiple training programs and successful businesses, Kasim proactively invests in transportation and vehicle leasing companies, cargo and shipping industries, agro-farming, and real estate businesses.

Kasim loves his work where he trains and teaches several people from various parts of the world about setting up a successful passive income through the online world. Apart from all this, he is a fashion and food connoisseur, philanthropist, voracious reader, and an avid lover of animals.

Through this eBook, Kasim aims to focus on helping his fellow readers on how to become a successful six-figure self-publishing entrepreneur. This eBook will further discuss his strategies, teachings, tips, and other insights related to becoming a successful author. You can find him on his **YouTube channel** aimed to help aspiring authors and enthusiasts who want to build their independent businesses for passive income.

For authors who are on the lookout for improving their business and learning new methods of promoting their work, this book is an ideal source of information and guidance. You will find some of the most influential methods, tips, and educational information for helping you succeed in this contemporary business of self-publishing.

Even if you are a beginner and have little information about this field, get ready to find phenomenal information related to publishing independently. This incredible career has been booming at an unstoppable pace. But, there are still some new updates that you will learn in this book. You will be introduced to ways in which famous authors have been writing, promoting, marketing, and distributing their priceless possessions among potential readers. In addition, you will also come across certain courses for getting you set on course to becoming a successful author. That said, let us begin this wonderful journey to gaining a six-figure passive income through your very own self-publishing business.

Chapter 1

What Self-Publishing Business Is All About?

All the books that you see online or offline surely have been published somewhere for you to enjoy. The method that encompasses printing these books has not been very easy for new and budding authors. The hardships of publishing were an inherent deterrent for the common person, until the birth of self-publishing.

Definition of Self-Publishing

Even though self-publishing incorporates a standard definition, it still works in a variation depending upon the context and usage.

For instance, you may look forward to publishing your book and pay for the expenses involving the cover design, formatting, editing, etc. Here, you are using the same steps as in a traditional publishing sequence, where the author completes all the processes involved and pays for all the expenses.

As you are the sole investor, covering the marketing, distribution, printing, etc., you are independently involved in publishing your book. Whether you complete all the processes on your own or hire a team, it is totally up to you. Thus, you are responsible for all the processes involved in publishing your book, without the help of a renowned publishing company.

Independent publishing will require you to be highly active in the publishing industry with complete management expertise and knowledge, as you are not involving an established publishing firm to help you.

On the other hand, there is also a self-publishing method where you take the help of a company. Even though the publishing company does the work, the author is paying for the entire process. So, here the firm takes care of the ISBN procedure, book cover layout, interior design, proofreading, marketing, and distribution with your investment.

Some companies will offer a print on demand service (POD) where both parties agree to print copies of the books in limited quantities and reprint when there is a rise in demand. This strategy is also practiced by big publishing companies to test the marketing and response of a new book launched in the market.

Thus, contemporary authors have a plethora of choices for publishing their masterpieces. Before moving further, you need to understand the differences between the two prominent publishing methods in a little more depth. You are going to learn their advantages and disadvantages so that you have a clear vision regarding their productivity and outcome.

Traditional Publishing

Here, the author will finish his/her manuscript, create a proposal or letter, and send all the necessary documents to the publishing company. In some cases, he/she may use the help of a literary agent to do the work for him/her. The editor of the publishing house goes through the content and decides whether it is fit for printing or not. Upon rejection, the author has the freedom to try his/her luck with some other company.

However, if the publishing house is ready to publish the piece, it proposes an agreement to purchase the publishing rights from the author and offers royalty for future orders. In this case, the firm decides the printing number for the copies and the marketing strategy for distributing the completed book.

Self-Publishing

In this process, the writer is himself/herself the sole publisher of his/her book. He/she has to proofread, edit, and gather the money needed for printing, designing, marketing, and distributing the book. He/she has complete responsibility for the written piece.

Previously, a self-publishing author had to create a set number of printable copies. In many instances, this resulted in several copies remaining unsold. But, with the privileges of the POD process, a self-publisher can now print a smaller number of copies at the start and keep reprinting them as per reader demands.

Basic Differences Between Traditional Publishing and Self-Publishing

Here are the various factors that differentiate the processes, advantages, and disadvantages of the two fundamental forms of publishing.

- **Time**

In traditional publishing, time is a considerable factor. Your book can take several years to print and distribute for selling purpose. This delay is usually because an author has to look for a publishing house that is ready to publish their manuscript in the first place. Expect further time consumption because of the multiple editing and proofreading sequences at the firms, which can take up additional months. Whether you have a fiction or non-fiction, the publisher also decides the time consumption for the final piece. Therefore, you can expect a couple of years for it - give or take.

On the contrary, a self-publishing process is much faster as the author has complete control over the process. This process can take six months or less to complete - depending on the writer. The best part is that books nowadays don't have to be a paperback or hardcover. EBooks are the latest trend that offer independent authors complete freedom of publishing their masterpieces in just a couple of days.

• **Finance**

All types of publishing processes require money. For traditional publishing, it is easier as the publishing firm pays the author if they are ready to print the book. As compensation, big printing firms may even offer an advance that may be a small amount or even six-figures. In addition, traditional publishing houses also have contacts, knowledge, experience, and various resources to help market the book properly.

On the other hand, self-publishing requires the author to create, print, edit, market, and distribute the book on his/her own. Surely, that involves the author's own expenses from top to bottom. So, depending upon the self-publishing company you are choosing for your book, you can incur heavy expenses. But, people who are great at all these processes on their own can save money as well.

Regulations that You Need to Keep in Mind

When approaching a traditional publishing firm, an author may have to face several hardships. For instance, the editor may not like the piece created so he/she may refuse to publish it. Maybe he/she found the topic too boring, controversial, or unsuitable for the firm's current list. So, there are plenty of regulations involved and the author is not in control of them.

Self-publishing offers the writer the freedom to work on his/her own accord. He/she can publish the book without anyone's judgment or consent.

So, which one of them would you choose?

While the waiting period in the traditional one is high, it does take away more than half of the responsibility from your shoulders. Self-publishing, on the contrary, offers you speed and control over your product completely.

But, as mentioned above, money can be a problem in self-publishing books. That is where the digital platform comes in to support you.

Thanks to companies like Amazon, you have the advantage of publishing your written books independently. Amazon's subsidiary Kindle lets you publish your work in the form of eBooks within a few days time. If you want a quick turnaround, then this method is definitely your best bet.

And that is what this eBook will be exploring, so that you can avoid the negative parts on your journey to becoming a six-figure self-publishing celebrity author. You have the power of the internet, which has already produced tons of self-publishing millionaires.

Now, it is time for you to do the same. If you are an inspired, but struggling author, then it is time to become the master of your own destiny. Through this eBook, you are going to unlock the secrets of becoming a true master of self-publishing, who earns at least six figures.

But, here's the catch.

This eBook will only help you if you are ready to help yourself. This eBook demands your patience, dedication, and religious commitment towards understanding and following each of the concepts discussed below. If you are ready for that, then congratulations — you just jumped onto the roller coaster to becoming a successful and independent author.

Amazon Kindle Direct Publishing — A Brief History

We all know how big a player Amazon is in the world so far. The number one e-commerce company has multiple subsidiaries working 24/7 for its customers. It has 15 publishing imprints under its name, and Kindle Direct Publishing is one of them that focuses on self-publishing authors. The firm helps writers publish their work without spending huge sums of money.

With this vision, Amazon started Kindle Direct Publishing in the November 2007. This campaign was also a step to promote the e-commerce giant's new product Amazon Kindle, the digital eBook reading device.

When KDP (Kindle Direct Publishing) was going through its beta testing phase in the later months of 2007, Amazon started promoting renowned authors on its platform through ads and newsletters. With that, several products under KDP launched for millions of readers worldwide. The advent of eBooks has since risen, as this approach is far more flexible and dynamic than its hardcover or paperback counterpart. But, eBooks have since taken a new form, which is self-publishing.

The Potential Of Self-Publishing EBooks

EBooks started with an aggressive business opportunity for independent and renowned authors worldwide. But, since 2015, there has been a noted decline in digital products. People are apparently back into printed copies of the various books, which shows that eBooks may have lost their touch.

However, this is not completely true.

EBooks, whether self-published or not are continuing to attract readers. Reports suggest that America alone reads hundreds of millions of copies every year. Moreover, several million among these copies are digital ones that authors write and publish themselves without involving a traditional publishing house. They also have large followings backing their products.

In addition, the number one supporter of such authors in the contemporary world is the e-commerce giant that prints and markets their manuscripts. When you have the world's top company supporting your stories with their massive wealth, you should not feel nervous about starting your self-publishing business.

Rise of the Self-Publishing eBook Wave

While self-published authors are not acknowledged that often by renowned organizations like the New York Times reviewing community, they have still nailed a considerable amount of book sales. One of their most prominent ways of selling copies is through eBooks. These digital entities have provided a unique avenue, and through its help, several writers have already started earning full-time salaries.

Without the use of a traditional publisher, indie writers, and authors have created their own path to write, design, market, and distribute their unique content. Thus, they have lowered the expenses that are usually involved in traditional practices. By chopping off those extra costs, they are able to boost their revenue, and earn a decent amount through their talent, unbiased by the opinions of traditional editors and publishers. Moreover, the fact is that many independent and aspiring writers, authors and publishers are learning these tactics to understand the huge sales numbers involved in this scenario. So, they are choosing eBooks and other self-publishing methods to promote their work, ditching the conventional publishing strategy.

When Amazon first launched its Kindle Direct Publishing network, some writers and authors showed up with some promising results. The good thing was that not only renowned authors, but also some who were not even known to readers, were able to sell their books through the platform.

Gradually, the idea of self-publishing through KDP kick-started the career of several new authors. Thus, self-publishing platforms rose like an unstoppable wave letting several authors share their masterpieces in various genres like science fiction, fantasy, thriller, romance, etc. Think about how much they were able to earn through this portal. An average eBook on Amazon costs around $3. Top selling authors were able to sell books in hundreds of thousands. This resulted in generating six- figure incomes for them easily.

For instance, H.M. Ward, a renowned romance self-published author has been able to earn a seven-figure income through it. Plenty of sales came to her through Amazon alone. And, she is just one of many authors selling books there. Several other renowned authors are makings thousands of dollars through Amazon, IngramSpark, Draft2Digital and similar platforms, all thanks to self-publishing.

A reason self-published authors are able to sell more often is because their book prices are relatively lower than traditional ones. Plus, self-publishing websites provide authors with up to 70% royalties, which is almost triple the amount received through traditional publishing. This does not mean that traditional publishing is not rewarding, but it takes a lot of time to do so.

Chapter 2

Budgeting And Money Management For Your Self-Publishing Business Online

Your self-publishing online business is going to require you to manage time and money. Even though money is the primary thought that jumps into your mind, time is also significant. You must know the complexity of the publishing process. Whether you decide to take help from a self-publishing house, you are going to need to do certain parts of the publishing process yourself.

For instance, you are going to plan the marketing strategy for your selfpublishing project.

Considering the level of your budget, you may opt to start with promoting your work on free or affordable options, such as blogs, Goodreads, Facebook, and other social media platforms. While the budget is low in such cases, it will require a large investment of time. Moreover, you cannot expect immediate returns from this technique. Thus, it is important that you budget your time adequately.

As for marketing, a recommended approach is to hire a marketing expert so that he/she can market your book efficiently. Even the editing part may require help from an expert. Nevertheless, you will handle some of the processes, like keeping your social media accounts up to date.

So, here's what you need to understand:

Your money management strategy should not just focus on the total expenditure, but also how efficient your budget is. How good is your manuscript? Will it require heavy editing? Will there be a need to rewrite various chapters? Plenty of questions will enter your mind when you are preparing for your first book publishing.

The Importance Of Money Management In A Self-Publishing Business

It's important that you plan everything properly so that you do not run out of cash while your publishing process is underway. Imagine a scenario where you experience a sudden shortage of money at the marketing stage. Would that not ruin your self-publishing business before it even started?

Remember that it is better to postpone your book's release date instead of running out of money because your book is more likely to succeed when you invest enough money in its creation, publishing, and marketing.

Keeping in mind the significance of your self-publishing business budget, here is a detailed section about the costs you can incur when publishing and distributing your book on sites like Amazon.

Money and Time Management for the Various Sections of the Self-Publishing Process

Note that self-publishing may be free or cost thousands. As mentioned earlier, your costs will rise as you start using someone else's service. Similarly, you can decrease your costs by investing your own time to complete a particular stage yourself. For that, you may have to learn new skills and try completing the work on your own.

• **Writing**

This is going to be your first step towards a self-publishing business. Here you have two options to choose from:

You can either write your book yourself,

Or, you can get help from a ghostwriter or co-writer.

Remember that time is a valuable asset in this field. So, you can write yourself, if you can spare it. This will save you money. On the other hand, hiring a ghostwriter or collaborating with a co-writer will drain your wallet but shorten your investment period.

Another thing to note is that both methods may involve dividing royalties. Thus, it is important to sign an agreement with your hired ghostwriter/co-writer. This will ensure that you retain the full rights later to avoid lawsuits.

Skills that you are going to need for this part: A lot of patience, creativity, and writing.

For writing yourself, you will need the help of software, such as MS Office, Google Docs, etc. It is better to choose the cloud version for your software so that you can find your written content available from any mobile device or computer anywhere you are. This will also ensure that you do not lose our content during a mishap. So, expect costs for this particular resource as you will be buying such software to use its full potential. You may also prefer free options, such as Google Docs, Open Word, but those will have limited functionality. Nevertheless, these will get the job done too.

As you are going to type a lot, it may become boring or tiring for you. To deal with that, you can choose dictation applications such as

Dragon Naturally Speaking software, or Google Voice typing, etc. You can combine this software with a good-quality microphone to dictate your computer to type the sentence for you.

• Proofreading/Editing

Once you are finished with the writing part, your next step is to proofread and edit your manuscript. We recommend waiting a couple of days before going through your document so that your mind is fresh when going through the editing process. Read the document, and check each sentence until you feel satisfied with it.

Here you have two choices:

Hire an editor to proofread the manuscript for you,

Or, look for a critical partner or beta reader.

The editor will check your content's structure, style, plot, grammar, and other necessary aspects for polishing your piece as much as possible. Hiring one will involve money, so be ready to invest in this section if you are not good at proofreading or do not have the time for it. On the contrary, beta readers are free, but it may involve you finding someone capable of helping you with the manuscript.

• Cover Design

To make sure that your book looks stunning, you are going to need an impressive cover for it. A decent cover will increase the productivity of your authorship, aid your readers to know about your work, and increase your sales in online and offline stores. Keep in mind that a good book cover will entice your reader to purchase your book. After all, the cover is the first aspect of a book that is visible to the audience. So, design it in such a way that it shouts: "Read me, I am awesome!"

But, if you think that designing a book cover is all about choosing a picture, some colors, and fonts, then you are mistaken. The designing part will demand you to know certain skills, such as Illustrator, InDesign, Photoshop, etc. Again, you are going to have to make a choice here:

Learn Photoshop, etc. yourself and design your own cover.

Or, hire a capable designer to do it for you.

Again, there is a constraint involving time or money. Go for the former option if you have a low budget and have ample time to design your own book cover.

Keep in mind it that being a good writer does not mean that you are a good designer too. Even if you are, working on all the parts yourself may exhaust you. It may not bring out your best work. So, try lowering the burden upon you and assign designing to an expert if you feel like.

• Print layout/EBook conversion

You will have to sort your print layout either for eBook or for POD. For that, you will require a PDF format for the print version, and EPUB format for the online version. You can choose from a plethora of choices here. Select a suitable software, like Calibre, Sigil, etc., for the conversion process. Alternatively, you can hire someone (if you have money) from online platforms like Fiverr, Upwork, etc. Again, you have a choice here: choose to do it yourself, or hire a professional to lighten the work.

• ISBN Code

With the help of an ISBN number, you can identify a particular book edition. For instance, you will have to purchase a separate ISBN code for your print copy and eBook version. For traditional publishing, it is a mandatory feature. But, for self-publishing books, it is not a necessary requirement anymore.

Thus, you may never need an ISBN number for your eBook.

Furthermore, most self-publishing aides provide with their own unique identification numbers, such as Amazon and its ASIN code, PublishDrive and its PUI, etc. Nevertheless, any publisher who helps you with the self-publishing work will inform and guide you about the need of an ISBN. You may need to purchase one if you are planning to use it for your copies.

For print versions, you will still need an ISBN code for your book as most countries still consider it mandatory. Moreover, many bookstores will not accept your copy without an ISBN number. This standard identification number is crucial for stores so that they can keep track of various book versions available in the market, evaluate sales, and order depleted stocks when needed.

Here is an example to explain this:

For a hardcover and paperback book, you will need two different ISBNs. This will enable a bookstore to find out the edition that needs to be restocked for its customers. So, for printing a book, ISBN is a must worldwide!

• Distribution

Unless your book project is meant for yourself, you need to think about its distribution. You have plenty of methods of distributing it, such as via Amazon, local bookstores, etc. Some of these will cost you while others will be almost free.

For distributing eBooks, luckily there are not many expenses. Normally, you do not need any upfront money for eBook distribution. A few firms may still ask a small fee for distributing eBooks. Make sure that this company is a genuine and renowned one if you are planning to spend any money. A good business model can earn you around 50 to 75% of the royalties from the sales, so online distribution of soft copies is cheaper.

On the other hand, distributing a print copy will involve heavy investment. You will need to print tons of books and then spend on their shipping and storage. While a POD (print on demand) facility will reduce those expenses, the service will still cost you more than the eBook option. It is more like a subscription fee that you pay in advance to keep your distribution process up and running for potential readers.

Nevertheless, remember that the above methods are neither good nor bad. Your circumstances and demands may require you to choose either of these methods.

• **Marketing expenses**

Money management becomes trickier as one reaches towards the marketing section of their books. For marketing, several processes work together to help improve the visibility of your book. Creating a website, advertising on social media platforms, and spending money on book promotions: some of these activities require money. However, with a proper money management plan, you can make sure that your marketing costs are almost negligible. Of course, that will take time though, so it is important that you have enough time in advance for cost-free promotional activities.

Building your website is your first step in gaining popularity online. Here, either you can buy your own domain/hosting (which will be a small investment) or you can choose other hosting platforms like WordPress. You can also choose an Amazon author webpage for building your presence online.

Another way to gain visibility is by being active on all your social media pages. You are going to need a lot of time to build potential relationships with your friends and followers.

• Promotion

Remember to keep some amount for promotion. You are going to need all the help your wallet can offer so that you can speed up the promotional step and get your book in the limelight. Various platforms will demand varying amounts for promotion. But, you can start your book promotion with a few dollars on social media platforms, like Amazon, Facebook, etc.

AMS ads or Amazon-based ads are the holy grail for promoting your books. This eBook will cover a separate chapter for AMS ads later so that you can budget appropriately for promoting your books.

After all this, here is what you should know:

Is it possible to self-publish a book for free? Yes, you can do that. But, remember that it will take a little time. Nevertheless, you should always consider investing some money in those departments where you are weak or want to speed up the process.

Chapter 3

The Importance Of Profitable Keywords And Niches And How It Plays A Crucial Role In Your Self-Publishing Business

An aspect about why several self-publishers are still unknown is that Amazon, similar to Google, implements a search engine to locate and categorize books. All one needs to do is to type a keyword or phrase in the search bar, and Amazon will show a list of relevant results.

Thus, authors have a great marketing strategy available in the form of Amazon search results. If an author ensures that his/her books stay on the top of the search list, it will increase his/her chances of selling the book to potential readers.

However, the question is: what causes Amazon to select a particular book above others?

The reason behind it is based on the keywords you are planning to use.

When you add your book for sale in KDP, you have the opportunity to choose a maximum of seven keywords/phrases. These words will help rank your book when someone searches for it. While these words are not the only ones you will use for boosting your rankings, you are notifying Amazon that you are targeting these specific keywords relevant to your book. Thus, when someone searches with one or more of these keywords, your book shows up in the results.

Remember that the selected keywords are not just valid for these seven locations, but you have to utilize them when writing the book's subtitle and description as well. This way, you are not only aiming for Amazon's search results but also Google's search results.

Thus, you have another use for your chosen keywords. You can add a keyword such as "weight loss," which manages to gather millions of searches per month. But, that will also make it harder for your book to reach the top 10 or 20 copies on the site. This is because the keyword is too competitive. Most people around the world will search for a simple keyword, so you cannot simply use it for targeting your book, because you may never make it.

However, keywords have a magical ability in them.

You can be more specific with your targeted phrase and let it filter more results out of the way, thus increasing your chances of ranking at a higher place. In other words, you can modify your keyword to "weight loss without skipping meals," which may have a few thousand results compared to the other keyword. So, you see, there is a strategy involving the selection of keywords. It is important that you choose them correctly so as to rank higher for your targeted customers.

Finding The Best Keywords For Your Self-Publishing Book

This process is similar to keyword research that people usually do to rank their Google blog posts. Therefore, your strategy should involve choosing keywords that will end up generating lots of traffic targeted towards your book, but with little competition.

Before starting, understand that you should first learn the types of keywords you should not use.

- Your main targeted keyword should be in your title of the book, but you don't need to add that keyword in the other seven places provided for KDP. Your book autonomously ranks for the words used in the title as Amazon assumes that your book is about the title itself.

- Remember to avoid using qualifiers, such as top, best, etc. in the keywords.

- Avoid using price-related keywords, or adjectives, such as sale, new, etc. in the keywords.

You may use adjectives, such as 'best,' in the keywords to rank a blog post on Google, but it may not provide similar results if you use it for Amazon.

Try creating a list of keywords and phrases that apply to your book first. You can come up with 20 such words or phrases that connect to the topic of your book. Think of what you as a reader would search for. What problem would you aim to solve through your searched keywords?

Now, visit the search bar on Amazon, and change it to the Kindle department. Start searching each of your generated keywords one after the other.

When you start typing a keyword, you will notice that Amazon starts suggesting keyword phrases through a drop-down list. For instance, if you type in "weight loss," then Amazon may autocomplete the phrase with additional words like "weight loss for beginners," etc.

These suggestions are highlighted based on their popularity among other readers. It is a prudent method to find keywords which are relevant to your book. Remember to do this search in the incognito mode of your browser. This way, you will disable cookies from crawling your computer and collecting information. This is to ensure that Amazon doesn't track your past searches to suggest customized results. As you do not want the search results to display based on your past searches, you need to use this camouflaged mode for showing results relevant to traffic.

Make sure to utilize enough time on this, as the searches made by readers are great for generating traffic. You want to ensure that you choose the best keywords that will rank your book towards the top. Remember to balance the competition and search volume with the search results, evaluated by factors like best-seller rankings, etc. to locate the perfect keywords.

Thus, it is important that you select good keywords and niches for your self-published books on Amazon to help you keep progressing on this platform. In addition, it will help you generate continuous monthly sales. The research process may be long, but it is a significant step in the business involving selling your books on Amazon. Just note that Amazon is like a platform that follows certain rules. You have to benefit from those rules to achieve the desired results.

Which Keywords Should You Aim For And Steps To Establish Your Book's Presence

As you have read in the above sections - targeting keywords is important. It is now time to learn which keywords you should target. Without proper keywords, it is difficult to optimize your sales page on Amazon. Thus, you are going to practice certain steps that will help you research keywords for KDP. You should aim for keywords that people search for, but you also have to make sure that these keywords are not highly competitive. Remember that targeting a simple and competitive keyword will be like finding a needle in a haystack, so avoid that!

Once you have your keywords ready, your next step is to understand and practice the following ways that let Amazon's search engine identify your book's presence based on the searched keyword or phrase.

• Kindle Keywords and Phrases

As mentioned earlier, Kindle's keyword selection procedure involves choosing up to seven keywords that help in increasing the visibility of your self-published book. Once you have selected the keywords, Amazon considers them as your top priority keywords and aids in ranking your book based on them. This may catapult your book to the first page of the search results or the last, depending upon the competition faced by a certain keyword. But, these keywords not only help with the ranking of your book but also unlock various niches on the Kindle store that help to filter the competition even further. Thus, you need to choose your keywords or phrases wisely.

• Title

Your book's title is the primary factor that helps a person identify what is the purpose of your book. Thus, if a person types a phrase or keyword in the search bar, and your book's title apparently tends to have the exact same keyword, then there is a high probability that your book shows up on the top of the search page.

Additionally, the keywords that you choose for your book also help in targeting your book's title automatically. So, be careful when selecting the keyword and the title. This doesn't mean that you need to adjust your title to look like a keyword, but you can at least add the primary keyword somewhere in the title to help it rank effectively.

• Subtitle

Calm down if you feel frustrated about not being able to fit a keyword in your book title. You will always have a subtitle to experiment with.

Just create a sentence with the significant keywords you are targeting. Similar to the title, your subtitle lets Amazon know that your book is about a particular subject. Keep in mind that you should never overdo it. Stuffing keywords in the subtitle will only make a reader feel reluctant towards your book. Make sure your subtitle is as natural as possible.

• Description

If you are still struggling to fit a suitable keyword in the subtitle, fortunately, you have the description section of your Kindle book. This offers you up to 4000 characters to let your readers know more about your book in detail. Surely, that also gives you the benefit of adding your targeted keywords hassle-free.

Several fiction writers have been able to benefit from this description section, which helps their potential readers understand what their novels are all about. Furthermore, this has ended up popularizing some of the finest authors in the world of books.

• Sales Conversion

The fact is that Amazon is there to help display the most intoxicating, mesmerizing and attractive products for customers. And, which products have such qualities? Naturally, the ones that are able to generate the most sales conversions.

Like any company, Amazon wants to increase its sales. Thus, when someone locates your book by typing a keyword and buys your book, Amazon receives a signal. It lets the e-commerce giant know to select your book for the Kindle keyword ranks list. If people keep buying your book after searching for related keywords on the search bar, then your book may end up in the first place in rankings.

So, this gives you another strategy: instead of simply sending the link to your books, you can provide them with relevant keywords that will show your book in the results. That way, Amazon knows that your book needs to be among the top ranked.

Thus, you can see that optimizing keywords and niches can have a drastic effect on your book sales. Adding small changes to your book can strengthen sales in your self-publishing business. All you need is the proper guidance for learning how to choose keywords. Luckily, here is a **keywords course** to help you achieve that target. Check it out if you want to master the keyword placement and generation strategy.

Chapter 4

The Importance
Of Titles And Subtitles

It has been difficult for authors when it comes time to choosing the main title of their book. Creating a catchy title is so important for some that they even spend hundreds and thousands of dollars using title experts. But, as mentioned in the previous chapter, the title is not everything. A book's subtitle is also equally important.

The main title of a book is created to pique interest, catch attention, and create an impact with its readers. The rest of the burden is on the subtitle. Its responsibility is to let readers understand the subject of the book. In traditional publishing, editors and producers don't even bother going through a book if they find that a subtitle is missing. This happens because time is valuable to them, and such professionals cannot waste their time reading several pages just to understand what the book is going to be about. Moreover, they receive tons of books every month, which makes it even harder for them to decide which ones are good and which ones are not.

A similar scenario may occur with self-publishing authors. Readers going through various titles will want to understand the book's subject, which is possible by reading the subtitle of the book. So, both title and subtitle need to be clear, lucid, and obvious.

Here is an example to help you understand:

If you heard of the bestseller book Freakonomics by Stephen Dubner and Steven Levitt, you may wonder why the title is so unusual, hip, and clever. But, that intuitive approach for the title may still not help readers understand what the book is about if the subtitle would not have been there. The subtitle for the book reads: "A Rogue Economist Explores The Hidden Side Of Everything."

Without this subtitle to back up the main title, it would have been difficult for an editor to judge the purpose of the book. So, the combination of the primary title and the subtitle led to the success of the book. It turns out that a powerful title may not always tell the complete story to lure in readers. A subtitle needs to support it to have a better understanding of the niche, scenario, and the story in a book.

Tips For Creating Titles And Subtitles

Your method of creating titles and subtitles should involve the following points. Each of these points will aid in marketing campaigns for your book.

- Never leave your book with just a title. Always remember to add a subtitle as well.

- Add creativity to your title, but don't be excessive about it. Your main title should be more creative than the subtitle.

- Be very precise and particular about the information you share in the subtitle. Do not add in fillers to increase the words.

- Think of creating a headline for a press release when writing your subtitle. It needs to be short.

- If you have some knowledge of search engine optimization, then use it for creating the right phrases and keywords for your title and subtitle. It will help in increasing your book's visibility via organic searches.

Mind that your reader may not be too creative or intelligent to understand your play on words in the title. You need to make him/her understand what your book's subject and purpose is through a good and clear subtitle. Combining the magic of both of these components will surely give your book a headstart in the self-publishing business.

Chapter 5

The Importance
Of Juicy Appealing Covers

With a book cover, you are creating the first impression in your reader's minds. This strategy is important for marketing. If you have an unprofessional book cover, then you may not be able to achieve the desired sales conversions. So, it is crucial that your book cover is juicy and appealing.

Book writers usually focus on their manuscripts and less on appealing covers. Adding an impressive cover to your book makes it stand out so that it is more attractive to a potential reader. A good cover is about displaying feelings, instead of just telling what the book is about.

Due to the lack of proper knowledge about book covers, several books are not able to transmit the desired message. So, it is prudent that you make notes of what you want your cover design to look like. A combination of an attractive cover, impressive font style, and intuitive graphics will help you increase your book sales.

Remember that with the help of a cover, you can market your book efficiently. So, make sure to have ample time for your book cover design. Your chosen design should lure in people, offering them charm and intrigue so that they are not hesitant about purchasing it.

To understand this phenomenon related to book covers better, here is some information about a book cover design's role for a successful self-publishing business.

Role Of Book Cover Design

It is natural for readers to be attracted towards a nice-looking book cover. So, its role is super important for a successful book business. Here is an insight into the role of a book cover.

• Attracts a Buyer

Several books hit the market online and offline, which is why it is essential that you have a mind-blowing book cover. After all, your first impression is going to make a difference between a flop and a hit book. Your book cover needs to generate an urge in the minds of readers to learn more about what's inside it. Its cover should interact with the reader, letting him/her know that reading this book will surely be worth their attention and time.

• Good-Quality Binding has a Role too

Bookshelves have plenty of books stacked in them, which causes the binding of the books to compress due to pressure. This usually happens in the case of paperback books. When you have a hardcover binding, your book is able to stand out amongst the other books. It is able to express its design so that the reader can see it and be attracted to it. So, make sure that your book's binding is of good quality.

• Adding Book Reviews

Another technique to make the book cover informational to the reader is by adding a book review to it. These reviews offer experiences of other readers who have already read it. Adding a review that is in favor of the story inside the book will help other readers feel more attracted to it. It makes the book more compelling to potential readers.

• Adding a Glimpse of Your Book

Adding a short description of what your book will convey is also a great strategy to increase sales. You can create a note by adding an attractive scenario from your book. It should increase the curiosity of the reader so that he/she feels an urge to buy your book. Make sure not to overdo it with the passage. Just add enough information to leave unsolved questions for which a reader is intrigued to find answers. It is all about adding a hook to the paragraph so that the person interested in your book feels like grabbing a copy and reading it.

Note that your book cover is one of the top marketing factors that you can implement. You need to invest in it as you will need it in all possible marketing locations, such as your brochure layout, social media platform, your website, sales page of your book, and on your book as well.

Here are some necessary components for your book's cover design

• Typography

This art involves using text in an appealing, readable, and legible style in a particular language. You can find it everywhere: on books, product stickers, street signs, websites, etc. Your chosen typography can create a mesmerizing effect, which may end up building your self-publishing brand. Several readers purchase books as they feel a connection developed through the typography style. Thus, your typography needs to interact with your readers so that they can understand the tone of your story.

Fonts used in this art can be graphic, exotic, neutral, and casual depending upon the niche chosen for your book. Furthermore, your book needs to show a message, which can be possible through the type of typography fonts you choose. A beautifully-fabricated font can help readers judge the potential of your book. You may never know that your book ended up among bestsellers just because of the beautiful and artistic text used on its cover. But, there are also some practices you should avoid. For instance, explosive or dramatic fonts, which are hard to understand, will only create confusion.

• Selecting Images

The chosen image for your book cover design needs to be a kind of teaser that attracts the audience. Mind that the image should not be a spoiler. It should not reveal more than it needs to. These images are more than just forms of decoration for your book. They provide readers with a glimpse of what they can expect as they go through the book's chapters.

Furthermore, a powerful image will aid to link readers with your masterpiece. Also, it will create an effective perception in their minds before they even start reading. Your aim here is to get a brilliant graphic designer to help you design the cover of your book, where he/she makes an intoxicating image for emotionally linking readers to your story.

• Strategizing the Layout

Before adding the typography, image, etc., you need to first design the layout. If you feel confused about this part, then you can consult experts or refer to other popular books. Check out the pattern they use so that you have a better idea of how to place all the components on the book cover.

• Keeping Track of Your Niche's Characteristics

This tip involves keeping in mind that the cover you have designed is able to depict the characteristic aspects of your niche. If you go through other bestseller books in the same niche, you will see that they have followed a particular pattern for their chosen images, layouts, fonts, and color schemes. If you think of going off the beaten track with your own confused layout, then it may not attract readers. Furthermore, you may end up losing sales. So, make sure that you stick to the pattern followed as a standard to keep readers interested. If your created cover is able to target the right type of readers, then it will help increase sales for your book.

• Color Choice for Luring in Potential Readers

In one of the previous sections, there was a mention about adding proper colors to your cover so that your potential readers are attracted to your book. In fact, colors help convey the mood of the book that you have written. You have plenty of colors to choose from, which can highlight what your book represents. A happy theme may comprise of warm hues, while a dark theme may tend to add contrasting colors. Try researching with other books that have already been added to bookstores. See how they have been designed with various colors. In addition, it is crucial that you choose the color scheme based on your book's niche without affecting the text's readability. Select colors that are soothing to the eyes of the reader. Let him/her read the complete cover page without difficulties.

• Centralize the Image Linked to Your Story on the Cover

This strategy is great for authors who have a recurring image or symbol occurring in the story. Try implementing that image proficiently with the book cover design. For instance, if you have read Harry Potter books, you will see that each book had a titular symbol mentioned periodically in each part. Like the symbol of the "deathly hallows."

Use a similar strategy and fascinate your readers with your creativity. Let them feel a part of your story. Make them feel connected to your story.

• Add a Contrast Cover Design for Grabbing Attention

With contrast, you can improve the clarity of the message shown through the cover of the book. This technique helps permeate the mind of the reader so that the real meaning of the book is clear.

Keep in mind that following these techniques for ensuring the perfect book cover design can boost your sales. Also note that some of these techniques may not give you the desired output right from the start. You may need help from professionals or do enough research to overcome your nervousness. We recommend that you follow the methods used by other bestselling authors and combine them to create a balanced approach. Once you understand how it is done, and have also achieved a good cover design, you can start experimenting with it for more books in the future.

Chapter 6

Why Longer Books Are The Keys To Success In This Business?

It is natural for new self-publishing authors to try to follow feedback and expectations of their fellow readers to come up with book ideas. For that reason, they tend to write books keeping in mind what their readers want.

As an aspiring self-publishing author, you may have ended up with a dilemma of whether to keep your books long or short. The answer to this question totally depends upon the targeted readers. For instance, if you have written a 400-word book, you will need to make sure that your book is compelling enough for its readers. If someone reading your book feels bored in the middle and decides to quit reading it, then it will only end up with you losing a potential customer and follower.

The key to a successful book is to keep it long enough to entertain the audience, and short enough to ensure that nobody falls asleep while reading it. Nevertheless, the aim to write longer books can have a great impact on your fans.

Here's why:

- **They tend to increase your dedicated fan following**

This ideology depends upon how you are going to approach your book. If it is going to be a very long story, then you may want to create a series of books. That way, your potential readers will get to enjoy the story as it progresses little by little. Take the example of *Game of Thrones, Harry Potter, etc.* But, the chances of increasing a dedicated following depends upon how compelling your stories are. In fact, it does not even have to be a story. You can also end up with a series of tutorials to keep your fans glued to your work.

Moreover, many may not even consider short books as a book. They think:

- These books are not a suitable size.

- Their spine is quite thin.

- They are not very heavy and do not resemble an actual book.

- These books are not considered ambitious.

- They are not worth the money spent on them.

Surely, such ideas are more subjective than objective. Nevertheless, the idea of a longer book to read is enticing for hardcore readers. In the end, that is what books are about: dealing with the individual perception of stories, fiction or non-fiction.

Here is another take on this situation:

Although there are several niches where the length of a book is crucial for its success, it is a rare thing.

A book's length and its presentation, including the backstory, cover design graphics, title and subtitle, should all be based on quality work. You cannot simply repeat passages and paragraphs mentioning the same thing in different words throughout a book just to make it lengthy. That is not considered a quality output.

What you need is a quality story or concept, elaborated with the right words that convey individualism. If researched properly, you can come up with 200-400 pages easily in a book. And, people will admire your work that comprises of quality content.

Note that even traditional publishers usually do not consider books with less than 100 pages as ideal for publishing, with a few exceptions. You need to understand that a book can be made as long as you choose, as long as it is offering significant information. Moreover, it should keep a reader glued to the story until the very end. Long novels are resplendent, involving a story that is compelling and passionate. Readers do not want these types of novels to end. That is what you should aim for if you want to succeed in the self-publishing world.

It requires understanding what your readers want, along with exceptional writing skills. Not to mention, an expert editor to support your work is a plus. So, long books have a unique charm to them that can easily engulf your audience and make them worship your work if you have the talent to lure them.

If you feel that you are not able to come up with a good and lengthy story for your self-publishing project, then you may want to get help from a professional writer. To help you with that, here is a great **ghostwriting service** to get you started down the right track. You can also use this code: URBANKASSI to get a great discount on your first order.

Chapter 7

The Mindboggling Power of ACX
And Audiobooks

There is no doubt that books have an effective way of captivating readers to keep reading, but there is another intuitive method that has become mainstream in recent years. The world of Audiobooks and ACX has shifted the mindset of potential readers in new directions.

For those of you who are not aware of this, ACX or Audiobook Creation Exchange lets you convert your written books into audiobooks. So, this gives you the power to promote and sell your book with twice the profits. This fast-paced method is a blend of technology and creativity that lets people experience fictional and non-fictional content like never before!

ACX and audiobooks have something for every type of person. Whether you are a narrator, publisher or author, AC creates a potentially lucrative, creative and better life.

Through ACX, you can manage the distribution rights for your audiobooks and get paid periodically for royalties. Thus, you are in control of your books with ACX. Millions of listeners are already using this new creative way of listening to books, which makes it easier to sell books online.

But, why audiobooks? Let's find out!

Reasons Why You Need To Convert Your Book to An Audiobook

Audiobooks are trending. You cannot deny the fact that the contemporary world is all about competition, proactive lives, and limited time. Top players in the business world are so busy in their lives that they barely have time for other activities, like reading books. So, how do they keep themselves updated and entertained with books? The answer is audiobooks.

These innovative pieces of audio comprise of books converted to digital files so that people can listen to their favorite books while multitasking. So, that is one of the reasons why you should get your books converted to audiobooks as well. Besides this, here are a few more reasons to choose audiobooks.

• The Audiobook Industry is Flourishing More than Ever

In December 2004, the Audio Publishers Association evaluated the size of the audiobook industry, and it turned out to be around $800 million. And ever since, the sales growth of this industry has increased to new heights with so many new sites with audiobook support, such as iTunes, Audible, etc. Take note that this popularity and net worth was back in 2004. And, this is Q4 2018, and the industry is still growing! It has definitely reached over a billion dollars by now. Do the math!

• Connoisseurs Prefer Audiobooks

Connoisseurs are experts in their fields. When you ask of where they got to learn about various fields and became experts in them, you will discover that they prefer reading books and learning new things fast. For that, their best bet is an audiobook. After all, who wants to keep glued to a book for information, when he/she can listen to an audiobook instead? It will let them multitask without wasting time.

This allows people to listen to audiobooks while cooking, working out, or driving. Busy people want to absorb as much as possible so that they can add more information to their overall knowledge. And that is how they succeed in life.

• Easy to Grab

Think of an awesome book that you have created for your fellow readers. It has already become a bestselling copy, and people are all over it. Demand for getting a copy of your book has increased so much that you are out of printed versions for them. Countering their frustration of not being able to get a copy will frustrate you as well. To avoid such a situation, an audiobook would be a great aide in this scenario. Surely, you have eBooks for them as well, but it is never a bad idea to have another substitute to printed versions now is it? With audiobooks that are downloadable anytime and anywhere, you will never run out of stock of your self-published books.

• Audiobooks Help Increase Printed Book Sales

If people find your audiobook lovable, then they often try going to a store (offline or online) to get a printed version of your book. They do it so they can add it to their library at home and flaunt it. Thus, you are not only making money through your audiobook but also through the printed version if people purchase it based on feedback from the audio one.

• Great for People who do not Like to Read

Millions of people around the world prefer to listen over reading. You can target such non-reading folks through audiobooks. Maybe they are slow readers, dyslexic or blind. Giving them an opportunity to listen to great books can help you to contribute to that community as well. With audiobooks, you are targeting more customers around the world, thus giving you a bigger share of the pie. Not to mention, many executive- level spokespeople nowadays prefer audiobooks too. They are too busy to spare time to read, so these audible options are advantageous for them.

• Audiobooks Make You Easily Accessible

While the audiobook industry is huge, it is still at a budding stage compared to eBooks and printed books online. With limited renowned platforms for audiobooks, you have a better chance of being noticed in such areas. Many times, people want to find an audio version of a book which they find interesting, but they cannot. So, this may limit the extra sales for such an author who did not care to get an audiobook conversion created.

To avoid such situations, an audiobook would be a great investment to help create a boosted business opportunity for you. You may never know when one of the connoisseurs, who may pick up your audiobook, may endorse it for you.

• Audiobooks are Affordable and Flexible

Back in the 2000s, audiobooks were quite expensive to make, mostly because of the considerable amount of time it took to make them. Back then, only the most renowned authors, who had lots of money to invest, used to get their books converted for their fans. But, with ACX and similar platforms, audiobooks have become more mainstream. It has become flexible and cheap, which makes it even more accessible for aspiring self-publishing authors. ACX even provides you an opportunity to get your book converted to an audio version for free. However, there is a catch: you will have to divide the profits between you and the hired narrator.

Remember that many publishers still provide you with an audiobook through the old way, which is expensive. While you get your audiobook, these publishers retain the audio rights even though they are charging you for it. You need to avoid such a situation by choosing modern services such as ACX to help you create your audiobooks with complete rights. Audiobooks can help expand your self-publishing book business to untainted heights. Think of it as a low-cost investment that will provide you with unlimited profits if done the right way. Here is an interesting and profitable **audiobook course** that can help you flourish in the world of self-publishing.

Chapter 8

The Art of Writing Powerful Juicy Descriptions

With your cover and title ready, you now need to give all your focus to the description of your book.

The description of your book is a short paragraph, which is printed on the book's back cover. It is extremely important to write this paragraph with crisp words.

This chapter will explain the art of writing a powerful and juicy description.

So, let's begin!

Why The Description Of Your Book Is So Important

When a potential buyer looks at your book, he or she can't comprehensively judge the content in the book just by looking at the title or the cover. A potential buyer requires a small gist of what your book is all about. The description becomes that helpful gist. A person can read and understand the core idea of a book. This allows the reader to decide whether a book is suitable for him/her or not.

Believe it or not, descriptions have actually changed the game of book sales in many cases. There are many cases when a book wasn't getting sales even with great reviews and beautiful covers. However, when the flaws in its description were resolved, the sales increased dramatically.

Such cases are pretty common in the business of book sales. Readers look at the description section to get a solid idea of whether a book is suitable for them or not. So, getting the description correct is key to consistent sales. A good description automates sales. And, at the same time, a bad description ruins the chances of success of a good book.

People out there want a clear reason why they should invest their time and money in your book. Give them a good reason with the help of a powerful description and you will skyrocket your sales.

Steps To Writing The Description Of Your Book

Every person has a logical side and an emotional side. A well-written description taps the best-suited side, depending on the kind of book you have.

Generally, a powerful description contains different emotions and logic together. Using the correct words in the correct combination can create a powerful impact.

There are certain steps to impressing readers with a well-written description.

1. Hook - Grabbing reader's attention with the 1st sentence

When writing the first sentence of your book's description, you need to ask yourself some questions.

What is the most intriguing idea of my book?

What is the boldest statement I can make regarding my book?

How can I drive a sensation in the mind of the reader with this one sentence?

People in life try to divert their attention as quickly as possible. The search for more options doesn't allow people to give too much time to one thing. So, if you are unable to hold their attention with your first statement, they won't read the rest of the description.

The first thing you write about your book has to be a compelling idea. You can make a bold claim, but only within the boundaries of your book. Only write what you can actually deliver in the book.

For example, a book description can start with something like this:

"Stop following the traditional idea of retirement in this unpredictable economy. Now, you have all the reasons to follow your life's dreams."

If you look at the above-mentioned description, it claims that the reader has no need to wait for retirement to follow their dreams. It also gives a hint that the book will help in finding reasons why the traditional idea of retirement is outdated. So, the reader is more likely to feel excited and curious to read the content after reading this description.

Similarly, you can write a strong hook line for your book's description.

- Think of the most compelling thought about your book.

- Write that thought in one sentence.

- Make 10 hook sentences with the same thought.

- Choose one that best describes your compelling thought and seems intriguing.

With that, a reader won't just leave the book after reading the first sentence in the description. Your first statement will give him/her all the reasons to give more time to the book before making a purchase decision.

2. Pain - Acknowledging an unsolved problem in the reader's life

After gaining the reader's attention, the next task is to highlight an unsolved problem in the readers' life.

Why?!

The basic rule of purchase is that the purchased item provides a solution to an existing problem. No person buys things, especially books, for no reason. In fact, the solution to a problem is what makes a book interesting and entertaining for readers.

When writing this section of your description, you have to focus on attaining the following objectives:

- Accuracy

- Reality

Whatever problem you present in front of your readers, it has to be accurate and realistic.

For example,

> "Your limited income gets in the way of gaining financial freedom, traveling the world and living more."

Now, this given statement directly hits the sore point of any person looking for financial freedom. The facts presented in the statement are accurate. Almost every person, who is looking for financial freedom, desires to work less, travel more and spend more time with his/her family. But the problem of limited income doesn't let it happen.

The same example also conveys how realistically you can present a problem. If the problems of financial freedom were connected to the unpredictable economy, it wouldn't have impacted the reality of a reader. But the connection between financial freedom and a limited income makes it a real problem for the reader.

That's what accuracy and reality mean in this section.

When writing the pain section, you can think about the core problems of readers, which you can solve with your book.

What are the unsolved issues in the life of your readers?

Do they have goals and aspirations yet to achieve in their lives?

Find those pain points and present them in direct and simple language. There's no need for you to be too much gratuitous. Keep your language as plain as possible. Just hit the reality and accuracy of a problem.

3. Pleasure - Presenting your book as a solution

After highlighting the pain, it's your responsibility to make the readers feel happy. So, providing a solution for the pain is the next step in writing a book description. You have already attained the attention of the reader. Now you can connect that attention to the book's content. Tell them what the reader will attain after reading your book.

Remember, this section is not about promoting a process. It's about promoting the end result, so focus on the benefits rather than the process.

For example,

"Being happy and rich with financial freedom is possible with the life blueprint you will find in this book."

Now, when writing this section, you need to make "clarity of benefits" an objective. Use obvious terms to sell the benefit of reading your book. Present how the book can completely remove a particular problem from the life of a reader.

With a clear presentation of benefit, you will successfully please a potential buyer. Here's how you should write this section:

- Write down 1 or 2 core benefits of your book.

- Create 2 sentences about the concept of your book.

- Choose simple words in a compelling manner to blend the benefits with the concept of your book.

- Give a few finishing touches to adjust the flow.

There is no need to use complicated words or make bold promises. You have clearly articulated the problem in the pain section. Just follow the same path and use simple words to connect the solution of those problems with your book.

4. Authority - Presenting expertise to the readers

A short but important section of a description is highlighting the credibility of the author, the book, or both. This section allows readers to understand the legitimacy of the book. They make up their mind that the author is an expert on the topic, so it's logical to listen to what he or she says in the book.

In many descriptions, the authority section also becomes a part of the "hook" sentence. You can choose to highlight an interesting fact about your book in the hook section.

For example,

> "NYT Bestselling travel book"

> "From the renowned author of [a previous popular book]"

> "From an award-winning financial expert comes this book on modern financial freedom."

This section stays short, usually a small sentence or a phrase. But it allows the readers to strengthen their belief in the book and the author who has written the book.

No one wants to listen to random people preaching without having any actual experience on that topic. People look for expertise so that they can follow a previously walked path to ensure success in the end. With an authority section in the description, you give your readers a legitimate reason to feel assured about the results you are promising.

All in all, this section is about strengthening the claims you make.

5. Open End - Leaving a secret sauce to generate curiosity

Until now, you have highlighted a problem or a question. Plus, you have also given a clear solution to that problem in the form of your book. But, there's one thing still missing - one sentence that gives a sense that your book has some secret sauce inside. This feeling is what excites the reader to want more and purchase the book.

Your reader should want to learn what's inside the book. And the content in your book should seem like some secret or a treasure. This feeling is generated by giving an open end.

For example,

"Your business is the most cherished dream of yours and [the name of the book] has all the tools to turn that dream into a reality."

See, how this example presents the book as a tool for business success but doesn't explain what those tools are. That's what you need to accomplish. Surely, you need to present the book as a solution, but don't go into detail. In fact, choose words that create a sense of secrecy. So, you can skip the "how" part of the problem resolution. This way, a reader feels compelled to read the whole book to find out what's inside.

This section is tricky to create. For many books, such as self-help, motivational, how-to and others, readers desire a basic idea of "how" they will get the promised results. So, you have to find a balance of what you explain and how you generate an interest.

At the same time, make sure that readers don't feel confused trying to understand the key point. Give the basics and include a sense of secrecy to push the purchase.

So, now you have the 5 core steps of writing a powerful, juicy description for your book. However, you will find 5 different sections of sentences after completing the given process. The last process is aligning all 5 sections in a smooth way to create a seamless transition from hook to pain, to pleasure and so on.

Tips To Get Description Right

The foundational steps give you a high-quality description to attach to the back cover. However, there are many things you can do to enhance the quality. Actually, the steps of hook, pain, and so on provide the purposes you need to accomplish. Beyond that, you can also think about the words you include, the size of your paragraph, and getting a professional to do it for you.

Here, we will discuss a few tips to get your description right:

1.   Shift your mindset from summary to advertising

It is easy to write all amazing things about your book in the description. You have invested a great deal of time and effort in the book, so the book itself can become your focus. But that won't help you achieve the purpose of a description.

The description is not a summary, it is an advertisement to entice readers to purchase the book. Keep that thought in mind at every step of writing the description. Don't give in to the urge to write more and more about the book. Stick to the promotional aspect and highlight according to the steps offered earlier.

Your book's description should work exactly the way a movie trailer works. A trailer of a movie creates excitement about the movie but

doesn't give away the whole concept of the movie. Only an overview of the plot is presented to generate the right kind of audiences. That's exactly what you need to do with the description you write for your book.

2.   Choose keywords smartly

In the digital world, keywords are everything. If you choose correct and relevant keywords, it can bring forward the right traffic, ie. people who would actually be interested in buying your book. Hence, you can't just rely on being accurate. Pick keywords that best describe the book and also think about the traffic quantity.

When selecting and including keywords in your description, you have to think about traffic quality and traffic quantity together. The quality describes the type of readers who reach your book. For instance, if you are writing a book on establishing a business, you would want young entrepreneurs, business students, and even business teachers to find your book. The quality of traffic increases the chances of sales.

At the same time, you also want to pick keywords that can offer high traffic. Which is why you need to find high traffic words in the selected relevant keywords and include them in the description of your book.

When adding keywords, it's important to not overdo it or force it in any manner. The emotional appeal and compelling nature of words matter the most. If you can balance that with the right keywords, that's amazing!

3.   Don't go overboard with the word count

As you already know, readers are in a hurry to move on and find the next best thing. So, you can't expect them to sit and read a large chunk of words in your book's description. It has to be appealing and short.

If you look at the bestsellers at Amazon, most books contain a short description, not more than 200 words. Some descriptions contain one paragraph, while others include two, or three.

You have to say a lot to cover all the 5 purposes of hook, pain, and so on. But you don't have many sentences to do so. Hence, each sentence and every word matter. It has to be the finest articulation of advertising your book in a few words.

Usually, writers keep editing and improving their description to reach a crisp and compelling form. This can surely take a while, but the end result ensures the success of your book.

4.   Make it easy to understand

After writing a long book, even complex words and sentences on the same topic become simple to you. Which is why writers tend to create a complex description. You can think that your description is simple, but actually, it can feel really complicated to understand for a reader.

Each sentence in a description conveys a lot, so it is critical to use a simple writing style to offer clarity. Even then, you should test the copy of your description by allowing other people to read it. Make sure everything is easy to understand and that readers are getting exactly what you want to convey. You don't want to create any misconceptions with your description. Otherwise, it will lead to bad reviews in the future and a reduction in sales.

Simplicity in description writing comes from the choice of simple words and a smooth flow. You have to focus on both when writing. A few sentences may be enough to convey the message but try to maintain a balance with short sentences near longer ones.

5.   Use a third person voice

Authors usually know this, but the description of your book can't have the voice of the author. You should always choose an objective third person voice to convey the description.

The description should seem as if a publisher or a third person is describing the value of the book. It enhances the legitimacy of the book and looks professional at the same time.

Many times, the description includes an appreciation of the achievements of the author. So, including all the praises in the voice of the author doesn't seem very logical. At the same time, the content in a book contains its author's voice. The reader should feel excited to read the book to understand the point of view of the author. And that excitement is not possible if the description itself contains the voice of the author.

Keep that in mind and write the description with the voice of a third person.

6.   No comparisons with other books

Many times, a book's description becomes a battleground to prove that this book is better than another. Such comparisons can make you look insecure about the book you have written. Sure, in some cases, a quote can automatically compare your book with some other book. But that's okay! Don't try to deliberately compare your book with others. Authors do this to clarify the type of book they've writtten. They think that comparing with an existing book will make their own book clear to readers. But that's not always true.

What if a reader doesn't like the book you are comparing yours with?! In that case, you lose a potential buyer. So, never make this mistake. Be confident about what you are publishing and present it with honesty.

7.   Get someone else to write it for you

In most cases, the author is not the best person to write a description of his or her own book. An author spends so much time writing a book that he or she becomes emotionally attached and too familiar with the material in the book. It's easy for them to focus more on the book's excellence, rather than the benefit it offers or the promotional aspect of the description.

That is why smart authors choose professional copywriters, a fellow author or a friend to create the description. Getting a skilled writer is the best option to have a perfectly written description. In this way, you can check all the necessary boxes and inspire people to purchase your book.

Now, you know all about the art of writing a powerful, juicy description for your book. To help you further with this, you can find this **effective course on descriptions**.

Chapter 9

The Power OF AMS Ads

AMS or Amazon Marketing Services, provide a kind of advertisement facility for authors who publish their books on Amazon and want to advertise them. These advertisements are presented to audiences on the search results of Amazon, product pages of Amazon and even on Kindles.

AMS provides different account and advertising options to authors. You can choose Sponsored Product advertisements or utilize Product Display ads. Both types are a little different from each other. They differ in terms of information, display location and behavior. Another type of advertisement includes the Headline Search advertisements.

So, within AMS, you have multiple ad options for your book:

1. Sponsored products

2. Product display

3. Headline search

Let's discuss all three types to understand their capacity to promote your book:

Sponsored Products Advertisement

If you choose sponsored product advertisements, Amazon helps with the keyword. Amazon analyzes the metadata of your published book and uses it to find more popular and relevant keywords. These keywords are usually the latest ones, which shoppers actually use to find similar books.

With that, you can start promoting your book. The location of such ads is the relevant search results. When shoppers type a similar keyword, they will see your book in the results page.

The goal of these ads is to enhance the reach of your product to targeted traffic. In this way, your book gets more conversions in terms of sales.

The minimum budget for daily advertisements is only $1 for this type of ad. Hence, it seems budget-friendly and effective at the same time.

Product Display Advertisement

With product display ads, you target potential buyers instead of focusing on specific traffic. Your book's ad appears on all pages which seem relevant to your book. For example, if your book is related to self-help, it can appear on all pages that contain self-help books.

The goal behind this type of advertisement is to reach potential buyers who have already become sure of their needs. Product display ads take your book straight to shoppers who already know that they need a selfhelp book. Hence, chances of conversion are increased to a greater extent.

The minimum budget for daily advertisements in this category is pretty high. You can start at $100 and go beyond as per your ROI.

Headline Search Advertisement

These types of ads are similar to the sponsored ones, but there is a key difference. The headline search ad of your book appears right on the top of the search results, not at the bottom. Which is why the level of engagement increases, which also makes such ad campaigns expensive too.

The goal here is obviously to gain a large amount of traffic from relevant search results.

The minimum budget for daily advertisement is $100, which can seem pretty expensive for many authors.

Most authors decide to go with the sponsored product ads due to the budget-friendly nature of that campaign.

What is the process of starting your own AMS sponsored product campaign?

You can address each advertisement as your campaign. And each campaign requires keywords. You provide about 1000 relevant keywords along with a price you want to utilize for that campaign. At the same time, your campaign competes with other similar ads to attain a prominent display location.

When utilizing keywords, you can use all 1000 keywords for one product. However, all keywords can work for all kinds of campaigns you design for your product.

Ad copy is another important aspect of starting your campaign. You can create and supply the ad copy, but it can't go beyond 150 characters. At the same time, you have to tackle several Amazon restrictions on things you claim in your ad copy. For example, calling your book a "bestseller" is not something everyone can do.

Amazon finds an image of your book from your listing and utilizes that image when displaying the ads. Every time, a person clicks on the displayed ad, Amazon charges the bid value. There are no charges for displaying the ad. However, the charges also have nothing to do with whether a shopper purchases your book or not.

You are free to decide your daily budget, which is the money you are ready to invest in advertisements on a daily basis.

How to Pick Useful Keywords For The AMS Campaign Of Your Book?

When it comes to picking keywords for such ad campaigns, you should research as much as possible. There are different locations and different techniques you can use to obtain better sales opportunities. Keywords and phrases related to your book are useful. At the same time, you can find cross-selling opportunities with some unique choices of keywords.

Here is how you can research and find keywords for your AMS campaign:

1. Research authors and titles in your genre

You are an expert in your zone. You have possibly spent years reading and writing the same genre of content. So, utilize that knowledge to find relevant authors and titles that are similar to your book. The readers of those books are more likely to show interest in your book as well. So, you can find keywords from the authors and titles of similar kinds of books.

2. Research popular buying behavior in your niche

If you reach the Amazon page of your book, you will find a section called "also-bought" there. This section shows all the relevant titles, authors and books that readers have liked most recently. From there, you can analyze the impact of keywords and phrases.

3. Research more keywords with the basic metadata keywords

You already have metadata keywords provided by Amazon. Use those keywords to research more. You can put your core keywords into book lists offered by Amazon. This search will give you a broad idea of what kind of books and titles are working. From there, you can find more keywords to include in your own list.

4. Research what people search for with MerchantWords

MerchantWords is a keyword tool provided by Amazon. You can type a merchant word, author's name, or a book's name to find how people have searched for those books or authors. Try multiple variations to gain more and more keywords to add to your own list.

Tips To Successfully Utilize AMS For High Returns On Investment

1. Define a smart budget

With smart investments, you can ensure high returns from AMS ads. You should define your ad campaigns differently with respect to the amount you want to invest. Advertising is actually the cost of selling your book. Hence, it's important to make sure that you always gain profit after selling a book. And that profit should exclude the amount you invest in advertising.

2. Stay aware of the latest trends in search results

You can't set an ad campaign and forget about it. The power of AMS works only if you keep your campaigns aligned with the latest trends in search results. Amazon is a vast platform where new authors and new books keep getting launched. Any book, which is relevant to your genre, should be visible to you.

For that, you need to constantly look for new trends in your niche and gather new keywords consistently. This will keep your keyword collection updated and allow your ads to gain maximum potential attention.

You can maintain a list of books and authors in your genre. Then, updating new releases and authors will become easier. And when the list of new releases become considerably long, you can spend one day researching new phrases and keywords using those new releases and include them in your pre-existing list of keywords.

3. Create and nourish multiple ad campaigns

An AMS ad campaign contains multiple variables in terms of copy, keywords, bids and many others. You have to test all those variables in different combinations. Try different copies and combine them with different sets of keywords. Also, try multiple bids to see how results differ. Keep an eye on the ratio of ACoS or Advertising cost of sales. This will tell you the sales generated from the bid you made.

With this approach, you can mix and match multiple campaigns for your book. It will lead to some bad campaigns and even some incredibly awesome campaigns. Now, pick those awesome campaigns and keep optimizing with the latest research. At the same time, remove campaigns with too high ACoS ratios.

You have to think like a businessman or a marketer here. In many situations, you have to choose whether to pause a campaign or completely remove it. Trying multiple sets of campaigns allows you to test your potential. Sure, you can make some mistakes, but you have to be comfortable with your ad budget to take necessary risks.

4. Give more importance to manual targeting instead of automatic targeting

Automatic targeting is a feature offered by Amazon to help you with your keywords. An algorithm checks the metadata and decides keywords suitable for your campaign. But there is no other person or algorithm who can understand your book better than you. So, you should give priority to manual targeting and research your keywords.

Mostly, manual targeting works better than automatic targeting. However, in some cases, automated targeting can work efficiently. You already know how to find keywords. Just utilize every step to enhance the potential of your ad campaigns. If you want, you can also try both kinds of targeting to see which one works best for you.

5. Be patient with your ad campaigns

If you keep making changes on a daily basis, no ad campaign will get enough time to offer results. It takes at least 8 to 10 days for ads to start giving results. Simple tweaks are fine, but you should give it at least 15 days before making any major change in your ads.

The Amazon algorithms can take some time to grab the campaign you have generated. At the same time, the reports of sales are generated a little after the actual purchase. The reports can have up to a 48 to 72 hour delay. So, if your book is purchased on a Monday, you might not be able to see it in the reports presented on the dashboard immediately. It may be visible by Wednesday or Thursday. This creates confusion because ad impressions, the KDP dashboard, click tally, CPC and ranking sections get updated almost instantly.

So, you should stay calm and give it enough time for reports to get generated and let the campaign show its true colors before changing your strategy.

6. Learn to gain insights from the data

Just looking at the impressions, CTR, and ACoS is not enough. You have to be able to gain insights from those numbers and make intelligent decisions.

For example, if you see high impressions, but the CTR is low, you can understand that there is something wrong with the ad copy. In that case, you can make the ad copy more enticing and engaging for potential buyers. Change the messaging and try multiple ones to see which one works for your campaign.

Similarly, if you see low impressions, it says a lot about your bids. Most likely, your bids are not able to compete with the competitors in your niche of marketing. Or, it can be a lack of relevant keywords. So, you can decide to rethink your keyword targeting and run a new research to find more effective keywords.

AMS is a powerful and effective way to promote your book and increase sales. It all comes down to trying multiple methods and making smart decisions to optimize new sales opportunities. Here is an **AMS ads course** to help you with the right approach to its successful implementation.

Chapter 10

VA and Swaps

Sometimes the workload in a self-publishing business is too much to handle and you cannot manage it on your own. Moreover, you may not be capable of performing all of the tasks by yourself. That is when the need of a virtual assistant is a must. Let's learn about who they are and how they can help you with your Kindle Publishing business.

What is a Virtual Assistant?

A virtual assistant or VA is a professional who can help you complete your projects and tasks without the need of being physically present around you. That means that the administrative expert can support you from his/her own home, a remote office or any other location around the world. Such individuals are usually proprietors who work online helping their employers.

For you, a Kindle self-publisher, a virtual assistant can help with:

- Gathering reviews for your self-published books.

- Posting your books to various social media groups and pages.

- Uploading your copies to the KDP platform on Amazon.

- Designing the cover of your book.

- Formatting your book to make it valid for Kindle and similar platforms.

- Modifying and converting the book cover for ACX and audiobook industry.

In short, a VA can help you with all the tasks related to your self-publishing business.

How Can A VA Aid You In Growing Your KDP Business?

Time is one of the most crucial resources that you have. Consider it to be more expensive than money itself. You can expand your business to earn more money, but your time will always be limited. You cannot make more time. Thus, it is important that you understand time's value.

Training VAs for helping you run your self-publishing business can be cumbersome without a proper mentor.

The average lifespan of a person nowadays is around 70 years. And, out of that time, you may have around 30 years to work and build your career. So, you need to shorten that time to become successful without working on useless tasks on your own.

Several folks try saving money on certain items in life by buying it from a cheaper place that may be a few miles away. But they do not realize that doing so is killing their valuable time. Instead, they could have utilized that time to make money and bought that item from a nearby location, as now they could have afforded it.

The point of this scenario is that you should not waste time on pointless activities and tasks. Instead, use a freelancing professional to be your virtual assistant. Why freelancing ones? Because they are cheaper than full-timers. You want them to do your work, but you still you need to invest smartly. So, VAs are worth the money.

But, will working on the project on your own not make you more money? You may be thinking that if you have no one to pay then you are keeping all shares for yourself. However, this is where you are wrong. While you feel like you are earning more here, you are just spending more of your time to complete the work on your own. This will limit your full potential.

Here is what you should do:

Try doing everything on your own initially so that you can understand and learn how it is done. Then, hire a VA and hand out the easier tasks to that person to let you focus on the more important ones. This technique can be applied to your self-publishing business as well. Writing the first few books on your own, with complete designing, printing, marketing, and distribution will teach you everything. Once you feel you have control over your business, you can hand over a few books to your VA to help you with the business.

VAs can Save You from Boredom

There are many times when you'll get bored of doing a repetitive task. That is where a virtual assistant steps in to take the boring work from you. In this way, you can distribute your work to have a better chance of earning more in lesser time.

Where To Find The Best Vas For Your KDP SelfPublishing Business?

For now, your best place to locate a proficient virtual assistant is on online freelancing platforms like Upwork and Fiverr. This modern-day community of self-employed professionals is your top place to get the most talented experts. Even more talented than full-time ones.

Such professionals know that their services are too good to be meant for just one company, which is why they prefer working as flexible helpers. You have a project that needs to be completed as soon as possible, then get one of the assistants to help you through either of these platforms. All you need to do is post a job with your budget, and several bids from reliable professionals will line up for you to select from.

Job Posting Tips to Hire Capable Virtual Assistants

To hire a good VA, you will first need to post a job on a freelancing platform. Here is how you are going to post a good job proposal. Remember to avoid mentioning about review swaps (swaps will be discussed later in this chapter) in your proposal as some freelancing websites like Upwork may not publish your proposal.

Here is a sample proposal to give you an idea:

KDP VIRTUAL ASSISTANT NEEDED

Hey, I would like some help for my online self-publishing business with marketing my books.

I would need the person to be experienced in this field.

Hoping to receive your proposal if you feel fit for this job.

Thankyou.

In this standard proposal, you may also ask the bidders to add their level of experience as a virtual assistant. This would greatly help you to shortlist the most capable one for the job.

Here are some questions you can use for screening them:

- *How long haveyou been working as a KDP promotion assistant?*

- *What other projects can you share with me related to this field?*

- *Are you working on any other similar projects currently?*

Using these types of questions will make it easier for bidders to communicate honestly. Try choosing the ones who have some experience to show for their work. But, remember that experienced ones may have a higher price too. If you are low on a budget, try hiring a fresher. Give them a small task as a trial to try out their skills. You can also motivate them by offering payment for the trial, as most professionals do not like to work free.

What Payment should You Set for Your Hired Virtual Assistant?

That mostly depends upon the level of the task as well as the level of the VA. For instance, a job involving review swaps may cost a few dollars per review. A job involving formatting the book for KDP may cost up to $25. Designing the cover of the book can also cost up to $20, depending upon the level of the designer. On the other hand, the remaining tasks may be on a per hour basis.

Whom Should You Consider Hiring?

This is a matter of quality as well as your budget. For books written in English, you are going to need assistants who are fluent in English. Native speakers may charge you more. Being on a tight budget, you may want to choose the next best option. Nevertheless, some fluent speakers are very good or even better than native speakers. The reason behind it is that they are too picky about speaking and writing grammatically correct English so as to flaunt their skills. Plus, they are more affordable.

Try countries where English is taught as a compulsory language to the citizens. Some examples of such countries are India, the Philippines, and some African countries. However, if you have a high budget, then there should not be a problem in hiring someone from USA, UK, Australia, New Zealand, etc.

Overall, you should aim for assistants who are friendly, disciplined, punctual, supportive, and understandable. Remember communication will be your top priority when hiring one of them as you might work with them from a different part of the world, so make sure to check on your time zones and mode of interaction to keep yourselves connected at all times.

Here is a quick tip for you:

Search for your very first VA at Fiverr. This platform has an interesting method of helping with projects. You can locate hundreds of thousands of professionals ready to assist you with any type of project that you have in mind. Use this platform to find any services at a very affordable price. Several of them have already worked as VAs for other clients there. Note that you can always ask for a portfolio of some kind to help you choose the right candidate.

Note that you cannot always do everything on your own. If you think that working on the complete book from start to finish is best for you, then you may not grow to your full potential. You will need someone to help you with expanding your business. Hiring a VA will free up a considerable amount of time for you, which you can then utilize for other important tasks. In the end, you will be happy to find that you just doubled your income.

Now, let's move to the section about Review Swaps.

A Brief Introduction to Review Swaps

One of the most significant components of KDP are reviews. You can consider them as important as keyword research. With a considerable number of reviews on your written books, you will be able to sell them more often.

To get that done, you have two options:

- Ask for favors from your potential readers and followers to download/buy your book and provide a review. (Note that this option only works for those who have a dedicated following.)

- Or, you can choose a review swap strategy where other KDP authors read your book and provide you with honest feedback.

This brings us to the unanswered question from before:

What are Review Swaps?

A review swap is an activity involving two publishers/authors, who both form a mutual agreement to swap their books and read them. After reading, both of them provide the other with an honest review for each other's work. For some, review swaps have earned a notorious reputation for being biased and unethical. But, if you plan on using it in a transparent way, they can be quite helpful for your self-publishing business.

The Ugly Truth about Review Swaps

If you ask other authors and publishers, you may hear them say that review swaps are fake and you should avoid them. Instead, they may suggest you to utilize your following to get feedback or let people buy your books and provide you with reviews organically.

But, such authors are missing one point. If you are not able to get any reviews on your books, then how will people purchase them? Readers prefer choosing books which they find popular. A reader may never touch a book that does not show even a single review. This is the ugly truth, which no one can avoid.

Plus, the ones who provide with such suggestions are already established publishers and internet marketers who have been present in the self-publishing field for several years.

Anyone who talks about using organic traffic may already have a huge following backing him/her up, so it is easier for them to say when budding self-publishers and authors face so many obstacles. Such professionals may have worked very hard to achieve their status and popularity, but they may have forgotten what it was like to be a new publisher/author, who does not even have a following.

Moreover, such authors also talk about generating followers without using Amazon. Surely the advice is great, but how will you do that?

A standard way of doing it would be by starting a blog and a podcast. Several fresh authors try to multitask their way by not only writing their first book, but also initiating podcasts, writing blogs, and promoting themselves on social media. And, they try to manage all of this while having a full-time job. One thing is clear — without sacrifice, you cannot have a piece of the pie.

While all these techniques will help you build a following gradually, it is not the fastest way to do it. You need to think in numbers. You will see that Amazon surely has what you are looking for and what you want to achieve. Successful authors may never try to disclose it publicly, but a majority of them target Amazon to accomplish their goals.

Famous Authors Use Paid Swap Reviews as Well

Believe it or not, famous and successful authors follow the same tactics for promoting their work too. James Patterson, one of the most successful self-published authors, followed a remarkable strategy to become successful. He would give a free copy of his new book to all his readers, and ask them to leave a review in return on Amazon. That is one of the many strategies which led to his immense success.

Amazon, on the other hand, ignores this, and why not? After all, the company is getting a huge share of the profit earned from Patterson's sold books. Now, imagine all the other famous authors who follow such tactics to fulfill their targets. So, remember that such biased tactics may also be helpful for your career even though they are against Amazon's rules and regulations.

You may think why they can they do it, but not you? Well, that's not true. You actually can! You too can apply such methods and get results at a much faster rate. Here is a small tutorial on how you can do it.

A Method for Doing Review Swaps for Your Books

This particular method involves using social media sites, such as Facebook. When you search for keywords like "Kindle Swap," you are provided with a list of groups and pages of communities sharing similar interests. Such communities are filled with virtual assistants, publishers, and authors that can provide you with review swap services.

Most of these groups are closed so you may need to ask for permission to join them. After joining, you can post your proposal there to let others know about your book. To help you with that, here is a sample proposal:

> *Hey, I have a new 99 cent / free book that requires swap reviews. I need X number of swap mates. DM me if you are interested in this.*

Others will see your post on the group wall, and the ones interested will reply back to you via a personal message. Then, you can message them the link to your book. In return, they will do the same. After this, you will need to sign up for a new Amazon account to swap reviews for your book.

Now, here is something you need to take care. Your network has a unique IP address that is traceable. Sites like Amazon will identify that you have multiple accounts, which you do not want to show. So, you may need to get yourself a virtual private network or VPN. A VPN lets you work anonymously without the need to change your PC or location. It is a way to camouflage your identity and location so that you are not trackable. Moreover, through a VPN, you can protect your computer from phishing, etc. So, it is a good option to stay safe online. While paid VPNs are worth the cash, you may still be lacking a potential budget to get one. So, you can try free methods like using Epic Browser, where you can hide your IP and location, and change it to any other place provided in their list.

After connecting yourself online through the VPN, you can sign up at Amazon. Using a USA-based address will offer more authenticity to your account. For adding details, you can create an address. A simple way to do that is by searching for a restaurant or cafe in the area where you want to show yourself from. Then, change the house number to create a new address from it. Now you will have a new address, identity, and location to start swapping reviews.

The Method to Swap Reviews

Now, that you have set up your account and identity, you will first need to purchase your swap mate's book. It may be for 0.99 cents or free, as per the listing. Download it, and wait for a day. After that read it, and try to grasp the subject, story, etc. of the book. Once you have understood that, wait for 2 to 3 days more and log in again to the account through the VPN server you used earlier. The reason you need to wait for several days is to make it look as genuine and organic as possible. After successfully logging in, leave a decent and unbiased review.

Remember that your activity should look natural. Otherwise, Amazon may flag and delete your reviews, thinking of them to be paid. If you just download someone's book and just left a review after a couple of minutes, Amazon will instantly know that your review is fake. Without a doubt, your review will be flagged. So, you need to work smartly here. Try being patient, and let this superb method worth in an ethical way.

Why be Ethical, You Ask?

Maintaining your business ethos will increase your reputation among your followers. If you don't find your swap mate's book that interesting, or if it is lacking somewhere, do not be afraid to share your honest opinion in the review. Likewise, you need to ask the other author to do the same for you as well. Just leaving five stars in the review may not be a good way to promote in this business. Learn to highlight mistakes and tolerate yours as well. Be respectful of each other's pride and dignity and work out a way to understand what you both will be writing for each other. Make sure to add pros and cons so that other readers will notice it in the comments, and find it helpful.

Going for a VA

This chapter already talked about the support of a good virtual assistant for this job. VAs can help with reviews as well. Ask them to leave their honest opinion about your book. Make sure that what they write is not plagiarized from somewhere. Their review needs to be original to avoid being flagged. Also, ensure that your hired VA is using a VPN to keep his/her account secure at all times while working for you.

So, if you follow these steps, you should not have any problem dealing with the promotion of your books. Remember that paid promotions are there. Authors all over the world do them. Some prefer by-hook- or-by-crook methods, while others keep it as genuine as possible. Ensure that you keep yours as unbiased as possible. Your image is in your hands. Do not ruin it by following crooked techniques. Show your passion for this business and do not just stay for the money. A built reputation may get destroyed in minutes. So, keep a check on it.

Chapter 11

The Game-changing Business Of Foreign Language Markets

Diversifying your self-publishing business is an exciting and huge step that independent authors use nowadays. Expanding your books in multiple languages lets you increase its potential to reach more readers around the world. Translation of books also lets readers explore some of the finest traditions, cultures, concepts, and ideologies that they may have been deprived of for so long. Maybe your book can change their outlook, but the language barrier had been holding it.

Foreign languages like Spanish, Italian, French, etc. are growing at a gradual pace. And, people from such countries are also interested in reading books, preferably in their own language. English may be the universal language to communicate, but that does not mean everyone speaks English around the world.

Did you know that the percentage of people who speak Spanish is greater than those who speak English? Is this not a good enough reason for you to get your book translated into other languages?

But, here is the catch. It is not just about translating words.

People may advise authors to write that they know. Naturally, that is what will come to any aspiring author's mind. They will try writing something they are familiar with. And, it does not matter if that written content involved extensive research or experience. But, what you may not know is that the content that may look familiar to you, may be completely oblivious to someone who is from a different culture, society, and background.

In addition, it may also mean that your content may mesmerize or fascinate the reader from other places. Similarly, it can be confusing for them too, or in the worst-case scenario, it can be offensive to them. So, simply writing about what you are familiar with is not how you should proceed in your book when you have an intention to translate it in another language. What you need to understand is the term localization.

This term has gained popularity in the business world to help people adapt to a new product presented in their local market. Translation is one of its main components, which makes it easier for people to connect with your books. When you diminish that language barrier, you are bringing a new community close to your work. So, your translation methods have to be good enough to blend in with the targeted audience's culture, tradition, and background.

Importance of text translation

Before moving on, you should know why it is important to translate your book.

Even though English is a universal language, it is only at the third rank on the list of the most widely used languages based on native speakers. Currently 360 million people speak English, but this is nothing compared to the numbers for the second and first most spoken languages. Thus, you need to understand the reasons for translating your book.

- **You need translation as everyone does not have English as his/her major language**

No doubt English is spoken everywhere, but the numbers are still less compared to other native languages in various countries. Surprisingly, countries like England, where English is the first language, also have minorities who prefer their native languages for speaking, reading and writing.

Moreover, even though a person is able to converse in English, it does not mean that they can use it for every situation in their life. For instance, a survey done by the European Commission in the year 2012 showed that only 3/4* of Europeans were able to understand basic English just enough to complete their daily routines. Note that basic communication in English is not the same as effective communication. That is why there is a need for translating books to give people more variety in their traditional languages.

- **People prefer translated books in their own languages**

Even though people speak English, they find it more comfortable to converse in their native language. Naturally, their preference of books is also in their native language. As an author, you do not have to provide your readers with books in the languages they speak and understand, but offer them books in the language they love from their heart.

Research has shown that people at a very young age tend to adapt to the languages they listen to firsthand, leading them to prefer it as their primary language of speaking, reading and writing. Even adults find their native language better than others. A research done by Common Sense Advisory showed that 75%o of customers choose books to read in their own language.

- **Translated books help you link to the world economy**

Translation services are growing for a reason. Even though English has been known as the leading global language for commercial purposes, interpreting and translating services remain significant around the world. Global communication is done through translators. Even political meetings involve translators. So, if global-level businesses require such services, why not a self-publishing author.

- **Languages emerge with booming markets**

Even though English is number one right now, it still does not take away language privileges from individual countries. People will always prefer speaking their mother tongue to communicate and read. Even their businesses are moving towards globalization in their own languages. For instance, many websites have content in multiple languages for bringing in more readers. Even Google has translation extensions for letting people understand content in various languages.

- **Translated text spreads information and ideas better**

With translation, it is easier to diversify various cultures around the world. People can understand translated text to learn about how other people think and perceive various aspects.

Here are a few examples to support this point:

Arabic language translators have been able to successfully keep the information shared by Greek philosophers alive to this day. This could not have been possible without them. Even the Bible, the Quran, and several other religious books have been translated in over 530+ languages, which has helped preach its philosophies and religious aspects throughout the world. Not to mention, world sports events like the Olympics all have translators to reduce the language barrier between the audience and sportspersons.

No doubt the English language has been an influential one for the whole world. But, it does not limit the existence of other popular languages like Spanish, Italian, etc. These languages will also flourish as time goes by, as people still like to remember their heritage and culture. Through their respective mother tongues, they feel connected with their own.

As an author, you need to understand and build that connection with your audience. Not just for the sake of selling, but also for influencing them with your ideologies and content.

Localizing Text

When literature is the primary concern, text translation is one of the most significant outlooks of localization. However, translation needs to be more than just converting it into another language. It needs to adapt to the structure, message, and tone of the locals of the targeted country to adapt it carefully. This is necessary so that there are no misunderstandings or confusions when people read the translated material. If you are not sure about translating it on your own, or if you do not know the language, then it is better to hire a professional translator to do it for you.

Hiring an expert who is capable in your written book's niche, will be helpful. Plus, it would be better if the professional is a native speaker of the language you are looking to target. He/she should also have an extensive familiarity with the culture, community, and traditions of the area. This is necessary so that your translated book is of high quality.

Why is it Worth Hiring an Expert Translator?

Your book translation will need comprehensive time to complete. But, note that some translation services can be really expensive. If you feel it is worth using their service then do so for expanding your book's reach.

Keep in mind that as an author you are not just trying to promote your work for a wider audience, but are also improving your reputation. You are trying to create a brand for yourself. A book that has been translated unprofessionally will only lead to a bad reputation. It can ruin your image, your sales, and overall reputation in the self-publishing industry.

Maybe your English version is great, but with a badly translated Spanish (or any other language version), you may lose readers from that market. Avoiding this situation is vital and you should ensure that your book translations in other languages is as good as it is in English.

Do note that hiring native speakers for translation is not always the best move. All native speakers are not efficient translators. Instead, focus on hiring someone who already has experience in translating. A cheaper option is choosing freelancing markets like Upwork and Fiverr to locate self-employed translators. They will be much cheaper than translating service companies. Plus, they will work solely for you while performing a gig.

Researching Your Targeted Market

Before entering a new market, you need to be sure to understand the fundamentals of the new locale. If you do not do that, chances are that your book translation may lead to a disaster. Just as when you researched for the English version of your book, you should follow the same level of extensive research for the other languages as well. You may also try to answer the following questions to strengthen your research.

Which titles can you compare your book to? What unique outlook does your book share with the audience? Who is your competition in your niche?

Such questions can help you target a new market better. Unless you are comfortable about answering all such questions for your book, you need to hire a professional translator to assist you. Following these techniques can be quite significant for the increased sales of your book in unexplored markets with different languages.

Chapter 12

Building Your Brand To Dominate
Your Niche

If you want to succeed in this business, you need to understand that churning a series of books is your way to dominate in your chosen niche. After experiencing some success with a book, it is time to move to the next step. You need that success as a catalyst to grab the attention of your customers, prospects, clients, etc. to gain even more fame and popularity.

Building up a brilliant plan to ensure robust success in the self-publishing business will help you implement and understand the endless triumph in your field. One such way of doing it is by targeting niche branding.

What is Niche Branding?

In the contemporary world, niche branding has a significant role to play for helping businesses succeed in the offline and online world. One of the key features of any business is the brand. Without the formation of a brand, audiences and buyers may not consider your business a legit one. As a self-published author, you need to set up your brand too. You need to show your authority in your selected niche so that people can follow you without doubting your work.

With this strategy, you are narrowing your brand to connect with your readers and followers. For that, you need to research a particular niche that will help readers. Your niche needs to target readers to solve their problems and guide them. It should not be aimed at the product (books) itself. You may feel that this technique is counter-productive but relax. You are using it in the long run to improve your brand's identity. Just as when bloggers try gaining niche authority to gain more followers and readers, authors too tend to target a series of books solely on a particular niche.

You can already see so many popular authors present in the world, who are known for their primary niche, such as Sidney Sheldon, Dan Brown, etc. When you brand your niche, you are communicating with your audience with detailed stories, guides, and exclusive information for which they tend to spend money.

People Follow like Sheep

Another fact that you cannot deny is that people tend to act like sheep at times. When they are clueless about something, they tend to follow wherever everyone else goes. Global identity can thus be strengthened through this unique capability of niche branding by giving people a reason to follow your work and buy your books.

Keep in mind that creating a self-publishing brand is not really about you, but it is about the category you target and the people who read your work. Churning a brand is about how your customers view you in the market. So, you need to aim at dominating your niche. And to do that, you need to control, influence, and define people's perception towards your work. Make your customers understand your content, and they will worship you.

Aiming Your Books towards the Contemporary Reader

Modern world readers are like connoisseurs who are connected, informed and aware of concepts. They themselves tend to influence others and express opinions to each other, which cannot be marketed effectively by traditional media-driven platforms. So, they cannot be fooled so easily, at least the class that loves to read.

And this community of readers is whom you want to target through your self-publishing business. So, using constructed and adaptable methods to win them over is important. To win, your brand should be able to communicate with people in multiple ways through your niche. In other words, if you are able to influence the audience through your work, targeting their problems and providing solutions, then you can become a victor.

Dominating your niche is a conventional method to segment your targeted market. Grouping customers in multiple groups will make it easier for you to focus your books in multiple ways. In this way, each customer will feel directly connected to your work. It will make each one feel like the book is meant exclusively for them.

Your Optimum Strategy for Brand Development

Any brand development is going to take up time and effort. Expect the same for your self-publishing business. You need to build focus towards your wants and needs to target various readers. For sculpting your brand, you need to understand which types of books you will write. In addition, you will need to have a clear insight into the features of your book. Here are a few things to keep in mind:

- Which age group are you planning to target through your book?

- What will be your signature way of introducing your content to readers?

- Which issues will you target and how will you try answering them?

- What will be your USP that helps you stand out against other competitive authors?

Some Advice for Your Self-Publishing Brand

For coming up with the best books possible, you need to understand your readers by being in their shoes. Think of what problems they are going through. Understand their desires so that you get a clear vision about what you are going to write in your books.

Once you are clear about that, focus on how you want to approach your book. Will it be a series? Will it be fiction or non-fiction? Will it be based on your life or some other character? Plenty of aspects come to mind, and you need to have clarity about it all before you start churning out books for your potential readers.

Building Your Relationship

Your books should be related to your readers, which is why they will be purchasing them. Don't forget that you are going to be successful through your followers and readers. So, connect with them. Let them recognize your work through your content. Create a prolonged impression over them so that your books can motivate them to achieve something in life. Doing that is only possible when you communicate with them through your written material. When you follow these techniques, you will start seeing results for all the effort that you have put into your work. You will witness that all of those who are within your target niche are supporting your work, thus bringing in more followers for you.

Things to Consider for Boosting Your Niche Brand

Strengthening your niche brand nowadays is much easier than it was before. With the power of the internet and intuitive resources, the world has become smaller. The result is that you can connect and communicate with anyone in any part of the world to build your relationship. This gives a better opportunity to sell to them.

Moreover, technological advancements have enabled enthusiastic readers to move to digital reading sources. No doubt there are people who love reading through a printed copy, but a major following is still actively choosing eBooks for quenching their thirst of reading. Thus, it is important to build a strong brand for giving such people a variety of interesting books to read.

In addition, you may need to improve the awareness of your brand. Here is some vital information to help you with that:

Innovative Methods to Increase Your Niche Brand's Awareness

If you have a trusted and solid brand developed for your niche, then you should be able to boost your self-publishing business. If you want your business to thrive, you are going to need to target your readers so that they can trust your brand. With that, you will be able to enhance your customer sales and base. Here are a couple of strategies to help you out with your self-publishing niche brand.

• Use help to promote your books

You can utilize a team of promoters to help you enhance the awareness of your brand, thus improving book sales. When such influencers, who already have an established number of trusted followers support your work, you can get your self-publishing brand's promotion done at a much faster rate. These people can help you promote your niche books through their established platforms, giving you their full support.

Some might do it free, while others may charge a fee for it. However, the result is that you are able to improve your visibility and get more potential readers to look out for your books.

• Influence others through motivational photos

Long gone are the days when all you needed for a photograph was your face. Nowadays, it is more about action, style, and personality. Being a great author is more than just writing books. You need to create a selfimage that will reflect your true self in front of your audience. When they feel influenced with your activities in the media, you are going to sell more books than you ever could have imagined. Mind that keeping a positive persona is important as you are going to affect your followers through your actions. So, be careful about that.

• Do not hesitate to meet your fans

Many times authors attend book conventions where they get to meet their fans and sign autographs, etc. If you have gained some popularity with your self-published book, you can be a part of such conventions to meet with your fans. Be true to yourself out there and meet every fan with excitement. Show them how much you appreciate them being there to see you. Even if there are a few people there to see you, do not be depressed about it. Your hard work, dedication, and love for your fans will pay off. Just keep working hard for it without feeling low. This kind of promotion will create a positive image among your followers and help support you even more.

• Be clear about your goals

Your brand awareness campaign needs to be clear and transparent towards your target audience. Do not hesitate to reveal what type of niches you are going to target. If your fans feel that you are being honest with them from the very beginning, they will support you throughout your career. The slightest dishonest behavior can cause your brand to become a mess. Clear goals for promoting your brand will also ensure complete trust over your work. That means, people will look forward to your next book when it is on the market to read. Would that not be a great way to help out your brand?

• Add video content to promote yourself

Another prominent way of improving your niche brand awareness is by communicating with your followers via a video stream. Use streaming platforms to discuss the release of your new book. Internet-based streaming channels nowadays are quite affordable to give your career a headstart. Try recording your own videos or get help from an expert to guide you through the procedure. It is definitely worth the effort.

• Create affiliate links to promote your book

Some authors generate affiliate links and promote their books by selling through affiliate programs, like Clickbank. This method is not that bad, but it is more about promoting your product than connecting with the audience. However, the content that you will use for promoting your work is going to influence your followers to try out your books. So, you will have to be good with words there to get them motivated. Or, you can contact other authors and work together to promote each other's books, like review swaps.

Surely, building a brand is important if you want to become a successful and independent author. Your self-publishing business may not succeed unless there is a good image backing you at all times. People trust those who are willing to offer their full dedication, honesty, integrity, and commitment to their readers. If you have such traits and are willing to work hard for it, then there is no stopping you from achieving your dreams to become a successful author.

Chapter 13

Email List and The Purpose Of Building One In Your Niche

With a major community of authors flocking towards the digital world and social media platforms to build a better platform for their self-publishing business, several of them are facing problems. Building a robust network, generating communities of potential interest, planning market sight prospects, all have to be dealt with when there is too much competition.

How are you supposed to handle the situation to keep your marketing and writing tasks up and running? Targeting all those people and attracting them towards your books is not easy. In fact, several authors who are not even regulars at blogging, social media platforms and other online methods can enhance the world, change people's lives or provide people with motivating stories. What is the solution to shorten the gap between readers and authors?

That is where building your email list comes into play. Any business needs to have a list, a directory of potential followers or customers who are always willing to support your work.

What Is The Purpose Of An Email List?

If you think that you do not require an email list, then it is possible that you will not need one. No matter how fruitful this list is, it may not be a prudent option for every author. For example, if you are working to become a novelist, but your published work is still pending, then it may be a daunting task to create a list, especially in a situation when you do not have an idea of the category of books you will write. Plus, you may also not be sure about which type of people you will be targeting to create a list.

However, most of the authors, whether self-published or traditionally published ones, need a productive email list to start marketing their work. Without a doubt, most marketing activities involved with this work need the help of social media. So, it is obvious that you need to understand the right way to regulate your email list through this contemporary network.

With social media, you can do the following:

- Locating readers in various communities.

- Engaging with other writers and readers.

- Evaluating the level of interest in your niche or topic generated among potential readers.

- Sculpting a community or group of followers who support you throughout your writing career.

- Ensuring that you are up to date with other developments in your field of work.

- Generating a strong response from your readers whenever you launch a new book.

You can find plenty of other ways to promote your work through social media. However, you will see that this may not be the best way of marketing your work and brand. Being social is not enough to boost your self-published book sales.

That is why structuring an email list is a prudent investment that will ensure direct contact with your subscribers. To give you a better idea of why you would need an email list, here are some reasons:

Purpose of Building an Email List:

Creating an email list for marketing has its own merits, as it is still one of the most preferred marketing tools in the industry. Emails are not just for self-publishing authors, but also for SAAS businesses, digital marketing experts, and various e-commerce websites.

So, here are a couple of reasons to help you understand that email list creation will be lucrative for your self-publishing business.

• *Reviving a Business with an Email List*

Many times you can lose your social media accounts, your blog, your website, and other digital possessions due to some technical difficulties. Nevertheless, you still have the power to keep your business active if you have a list of emails.

Several major authors keep their email list as their top resource to reach out to potential business prospects. In fact, many of them have set up multi-million dollar businesses based on the support of a powerful email list. Many have built most of their income by promoting their merchandise and books via emails. And, all this is possible without the need of keeping a check on social media accounts, etc.

• *Your Email List is Your Own*

Your social media accounts and rankings on search engine lists are all owned by multinational companies which can all be taken away from you due to some technical issues. However, your email list is completely private to you in your email account that is completely based on your personal information. Social media websites and rankings are mostly open to the public, so they are still visible to everyone, but not your email list.

• Communicating through an Email is Really Cheap

Sending emails is cheap. It is even cheaper (or free) if you are using a free account via Google, Yahoo, etc. Going for private companies to subscribe to a messaging plan will be way more expensive for you. On the other hand, emails are safe and cheap, period.

• People Find Emails more Feasible to Interact with and Purchase Things

Several bits of research have already supported this claim. Here are a few for you to understand:

Merkle, a renowned CRM (customer relationship management) company claimed that 74% of individuals present online tend to choose an email for communicating commercially.

*Building relations with customers is important for
a successful self-publishing business.*

Another agency by the name ExactTarget mentioned that email was ranked as the number one source for personal interaction. They mentioned that 77% of people used an email over other modes when it came to commercial messages. A reason behind this choice, as per the agency's survey was that people preferred receiving marketing interactions through prior permissions, which is possible via emails.

Another questionnaire with the Nielson Norman Group highlighted that 90% of their customers preferred receiving a newsletter via email. The remaining 10% read Facebook and other social media sites.

• *Emails are Affordable, Fast, and Easy to Send*

Email service agencies have enabled the network to become highly advanced so that it is easier to communicate, at a much faster rate. Several service providers that enhance emails to new levels of outlook now offer additional features. You can add beautiful templates, use drag-and-drop techniques, add links, create tables, and whatnot. It has all become quite easy, which gives you the tools to highlight your newsletters in a defined way for your potential customers. This all would not have been possible via other modes with such a fast output.

• *Communicating Regularly via Email Builds Trust for a Prolonged Period*

All business types are about building trust. People usually trust businessmen and service providers when they feel connected on a regular basis. That is where emails offer a segmented and customizable layout to connect with each and every customer directly. These newsletters personally target each reader, making him/her feel like the message was only written for him/her. After sharing a couple of emails with personalized messages, tips, and other useful information, your customers will start trusting you for advice. This may end up with them asking for your help or service eventually. Through emails, you can target your valuable content, and make sure that your customers find your information helpful for them.

• *Email Marketing is Customizable as per Individual Preferences*

Each email message that you create for your readers is easy to customize, optimize, segment, and test as per your wish. You can keep modifying the design and experiment with whatever is suitable for your customers. This ease of work makes it worth your time and effort.

• *Email Lists can be Highly Lucrative within a Couple of Hours*

If you know the right way of doing it, then you can easily earn decent sums through your email list. It is a matter of using the right techniques to sell your books or other products. If they are impressed, they will buy your books, courses, and other self-published material. Faithful followers in your email list can be contacted to earn fast cash by selling your products too. But, do not keep asking your readers to purchase things using this technique as it feels unethical at times.

• *Email is the Topmost Method for High ROI*

Salesforce, a popular CRM-based service provider noted that email marketing has a return on investment of 3800%. This is because over 80% of users still prefer emails for communicating commercially. Several surveys have been done to prove such numbers, which is why email marketing is a great way of promoting your business.

• *High Sustainability Over Time without the Need of Outside Resources*

With a growing email list, you will witness that a considerable amount of traffic that visits your website is from your emailed newsletters. With time, you will not need the help of search engine marketing tactics, etc. to keep your self-publishing business running.

Your referrals and email list will be sufficient to keep your business active.

• *Your Email List Acts as a Powerful Asset that You can Sell if You Like*

Internet companies and direct marketing campaigns have an impressive value for sale. Your website, inventory, and storage areas are all secondary as these will not get you direct customers. Your email list plays a role there as your list brings in valuable customers who trust you for information. So, there is a high chance that these followers in your list will purchase your recommended products.

Such a list can be very valuable to a buyer. Anyone who can benefit from your list will be willing to spend a decent sum to get it from you. So, you have the benefit of selling your list when you feel like.

Thus, you can see that you have a relevant purpose to create an email list, which is much more effective than other modes of promotion and communication with prospects.

Chapter 14

Importance Of Having Author Profile Pages Set

Any author needs to have a platform that informs his/her readers and followers about his/her work and existence. This is where an author profile comes into play with its stirring capabilities. You may have witnessed that some authors choose to promote themselves using a group or page on social media sites.

However, that is not a fruitful way of promoting your business. Instead of choosing a page, it is better to keep yourself active through a completed author profile. Before moving to why it is important to have an impressive author profile, you should first learn the difference between a page and profile.

A page is specifically meant to promote and sell a product or service. This may not always be the best way of communicating for growing authors. Your followers may start judging you over time. And, the result may not be productive.

On the other hand, an author profile will let you connect with your potential readers and followers at a ground level. It will be more like being their friend, where you can contact them personally to share insights into your upcoming books and projects. This way, they feel special, and the result is their prolonged connection and faith in your work.

Here is what readers prefer:

Any reader who loves an author's work will be interested in learning about the writer's life and process of writing. In addition, the reader may also be interested in firsthand news and updates on upcoming campaigns, convention meets, sales, new releases, etc. Moreover, readers or followers also love having access to meet their favorite authors, which are much more approachable through an author profile.

Remember that social media platforms, like Facebook, may have pages and groups for promotional aspects, but the real purpose of such a platform is to interact with friends. So, if you are planning to set up an author profile, then make sure to keep it as communicative with your followers as possible. This will help you grow your army of readers who are faithful to you.

To give you a better glimpse of what an author profile can do for you, here are some points to consider:

• *It's Easier to Present and Understand*

A majority of readers find it easier to connect with you through your author profile, instead of some other mode of marketing. Remember that you are not a corporation that runs his/her business hiding behind someone else's image. Be proud of your identity and do not feel reluctant to show yourself to your audience. Your followers will love to be a part of your community when they find that a person is there to always communicate with them.

With an author profile, you are offering yourself to your audience and letting them know that you are approachable. Through your profile, your readers will come to know you at a much better pace. Moreover, your profile is more organic compared to a page or group that is run with the sole purpose of marketing your products.

• *You Have Posts That Are More Visible*

Authors found that there are more chances of gaining visibility through posts shared on their profile instead of other modes. Consider this situation as an example:

If a popular author has a verified author profile on Facebook, his/her following will greatly increase as people will know of his/her authenticity. People nowadays know that the author does not necessarily run Facebook pages, etc. himself or herself. It is possible for them to ignore the author's page as they do not find themselves connected with him/her.

On the other hand, if an author updates through his or her profile, then people will have more faith in his or her work. Your profile will let you communicate with individual followers and friends, which increases the chances of building stronger bonds. This is not possible on community pages.

• *Much Simpler to Handle*

The backend work in a profile is much easier than in an author-marketing page. Your profile account will not require you to keep posting just for the sake of marketing. Furthermore, you do not even need to keep multiple groups when you are just organizing your author profile for sharing updates with your followers. This also limits any chances of confusions.

• *You Can Have Many More Features with a Profile Account*

Profile accounts let you get access to unlimited followers who genuinely support your work, but only when they find that it is your real account. Several celebrities nowadays prefer creating accounts instead of maintaining pages. This way, you are in control of posting every update on your own, which is viewable by the people who love your work.

So you can see that with the help of an author profile, you are a part of your followers yourself, instead of sitting high up in some royal chair waving at your audience below. Fans love to follow people whom they find generous and without an attitude. Seeing that you have an author profile will make them not judge your intentions. Once your connections with your followers is strong, you can occasionally share updates related to work and leisure, which your fans will love.

But, in all this situation, there is also a matter of congruency.

Congruency Between Self-Image And Brand Reputation

Building a relationship to solidify your brand image is not the same as self-image. Your brand mostly focuses on treating readers as customers. Thus, brand reputation is more about building customer relationships.

On the other hand, your self-image is based on your personal actions and activities that influence your potential readers and followers. Choosing either one of them will not provide you with the necessary results. There has to be a balance between these two methods to keep everyone satisfied.

Think of it like this:

You are an aspiring author who has recently completed a book. You are ready to start publishing it through a self-publishing platform. Your book is listed for purchase. However, you notice that nobody is even looking at your book. This is because you never built an image to promote yourself organically.

You did not care about improving your author profile that would have enabled you to influence your followers, so they could trust you before choosing your work as a daily dose of motivation or relaxation. Congruency between your self-image and brand image would have played a significant role as a combination.

Firstly, you would have needed to develop your author profile to enable potential followers and readers to connect with you. Once they felt that you are someone they can count on for advice, then you should have chosen to market your books. But, that also needs to be in a way that it is not biased.

Chapter 15

Expansion and Re-investing Into Your Business To Become A Successful Self-Publishing Entrepreneur

Any self-published author understands that he/she needs to give months and years of churning into his/her writing work before their first big break. Once an author is able to get his/her first book printed or published, he/she steps on the boat to become an entrepreneur. As an aspiring author, your self-publishing business will give you a platform, and from there is it up to you to choose your road to success.

You will have plenty of opportunities after placing your first book in the published section. But, after the first book, you will need to build a strategy to invest, re-invest and expand your business to a six-figure level at least. But, expansions requires investment at times.

One such way of expanding and re-investing is through crowdfunding.

This popular way of raising funds for budding authors is by seeking support of followers and fans. Several authors have already found this method fruitful for expanding their career.

When you look at it for the first time, you may think that it is quite an easy task: setting up a page on a crowdfunding network of your preferred niche, and watching people you do not even know lining up to invest in your work.

But, the situation is not your daily cup of tea.

According to several Kickstarter reports, most campaigns present on their site fail miserably. The firm reported that only 35% of these campaigns succeeded in their goals. The rest of them all failed.

This section is not to demotivate you in any way if you are planning to set up a crowdfunding page for your self-publishing business. In fact, you will learn some techniques to give yourself a headstart for becoming a successful author and running a lucrative business. The following three things will help you use crowdfunding for your self-published business.

• *Using Your Campaign for Marketing Religiously*

If you are setting up your crowdfunding campaign for just the purpose of acquiring funds, then it may not be a good idea to do so. You need to strategize your marketing tactics. For that, you are going to need to locate and connect with people who are interested in your work. Funds will automatically follow once you have impressed your potential fans and followers.

Several renowned authors have used crowdfunding platforms, like Kickstarter, to generate funds by building buzz and interest in the minds of people, even before their book publication.

Keep in mind that your crowdfunding campaign is a strategy that you are investing your time and effort in before the actual marketing. You are going to need a good plan to communicate with your audience. That is where your email list can also be handy, if you have one. Build your reputation so that your readers can reach out to you directly. Only then will they think of investing in your work.

• *You May Face Hurdles, but Do Not Back Out*

As mentioned earlier, several crowdfunding campaigns fail. The situation is even more despicable for the ones who do not even receive a single investor. That is where you should not give up. As a selfpublishing entrepreneur, you have chosen a road to sustenance that most people are too scared to take. But, if you have stepped on this boat to achieve success, then you cannot give up that easily.

Your first few campaigns may even fail to meet their goals, but that should not stop you from trying. Instead, figure out what made the situation fail. Try to find the errors and correct them for your next try. Choose a different angle to your purpose so that people can know you better. Let them see how good you are at your work. Be active on social media platforms to socialize with your audience. Then, you can approach them for your future goals of expansion and re-investment.

• *Keep Your Campaign Visually Attractive*

Any campaign looks more approachable when it is visually appealing. You should follow this strategy in your goals as well. Focus on the artwork to attract the crowd and let them witness the talent in you and your work. Your creativity should reflect your persona that engulfs your potential investors in a unique way. Choose videos, images, infographics, etc. to create a beautiful profile that no one can stop looking at. With time and effort, you will witness that your hard work has born fruitful results for helping you expand your self-publishing business.

The Purpose Of Reinvesting Your Earnings In Your Self-Publishing Business

For any business, working hard at accumulating wealth at a normal pace is not enough, unless you do not have ambitious dreams. However, as you are thinking of becoming a self-published author, you are going to need to keep your business expanding. For that, a sound reinvestment strategy is prudent.

Successful authors and bloggers have been able to achieve their current levels as they have been reinvesting a particular amount of their earnings back into their business. That is how things work for the ones who want to succeed in this industry. After all, crowdfunding may not always work. So, your investment resource may come from your earned wealth by selling books.

To give you a better idea, here is why reinvesting is one of the most significant tactics for your self-published business.

• *It Is Highly Lucrative for Faster Growth*

A majority of budding entrepreneurs initiate by saving the amount that their business earns, thinking of it as an income. The result is that the amount that they earn is spent on other activities. However, you need to rethink your strategy and invest some of that earned amount back into your business to grow it. If you are not reinvesting in your business regularly, you are just earning enough to sustain your life, which is not always a good move. Reinvesting in your business will enable you to expand to new heights. You will be able to grow your business exponentially in less time.

• *You Will Learn as You Grow*

Mind that all the investments that you will be making in your business may not necessarily succeed. You may lose money along the way. But, note that it is the way you will learn to improve in this field. Your mistakes will give you ways to improve in your self-publishing business. There will be times when you hire the wrong people to help you out, which may result in financial losses. However, the key is to not give up as you grow.

Each of your experiences will help you sort things out for the next strategy. In the end, you will have success in targeting your audience in an efficient way. You will have better chances of accumulating your invested wealth if you are cautious in your ways. So prepare yourself to make mistakes as you invest in your field. Even if you have success with your strategy, you may witness that not all investment choices are perfect. Keep a check on them too so that you can improve your work and spend smartly.

• *Running a Business Alone Is Tough*

If you run your business on your own, you may exhaust yourself. Selfpublishing businesses require so many tasks to be completed, which are impossible to handle alone. Even if you are doing it all yourself, you will not be able to grow your business as you will be too busy focusing on the tasks at hand.

To make your business move to the next level, you will need the help of capable contractors or freelancers to aid you in your business goals. This step can make you nervous at times as you are about to spend your hard-earned money with a vision to grow it. As mentioned earlier, you may witness failures too, but only if you are not careful with your strategy.

Thus, be careful while choosing a team to help you with your self-publishing business. You want it to grow to new levels where you are satisfied. A good way to manage it all is by doing the things you are good at yourself, and outsourcing the remaining tasks through hired professionals. You may feel uncomfortable allotting work to others, but remember that it is much easier to assign to others than doing it all yourself. After all, you are planning it all to expand your self-publishing business.

Tips for Publishing Your Own Book

More and more entrepreneurs are joining the self-publishing business and promoting their own brands. It may have been hard to do before, but now there are so many self-publishing platforms to aid you with the task. They may mostly come in the form of eBooks, but several firms are also providing printed versions nowadays. However, there are still issues involved with publishing your first book. To help you with that, you need to be aware of the following tips:

• *Choosing an Engaging Topic for Your Book*

As mentioned before, a niche is important to start with for your very first book. But, now let us learn about what topic to choose for your book. You may feel confused if you have multiple topics in mind. You may choose a generic topic if you are not targeting a particular niche. But, make sure to keep it balanced so that all types of readers can understand it. Getting too technical or too theoretical can lead to a negative impact. Keep in mind that your first book should be engaging enough to lure in a bigger audience. Even the word count of your book should be suitable enough for your work to look like a decent-sized book. So, keep note of that.

• *Learn the Basics*

Self-publishing has certain rules and regulations too. Make sure that you are aware of them to understand whether you are on the right track or not. For instance, an ISBN code may not be needed if you are going for just an eBook version of your book. On the other hand, a print version may require an ISBN. Look for other such rules and keep track of new updates as well while you are working on your book.

• *Keep a Check on Your Budget as Well*

Self-publishing may have a smaller budget compared to a traditional one, but it does not mean that you can do it without spending anything. Some tasks may require you to hire people too. For instance, if you are good at writing but not at designing, then you will need help from a professional. Nevertheless, your budget can be decided based on how much time you have for the book to be completed. If you are capable of handling all self-publishing tasks on your own, then you can do that, only if you have ample time for it.

• *Generate a Capable Marketing Strategy*

It is not necessary that your book is the best there is. But, that should not demotivate you from marketing it properly. Your marketing strategy should be impeccable. Use all the modes and resources you have for marketing your book to let people know about it. If you own a website, use it for promoting your work. But, make sure that you have a following to promote yourself. If people do not know about you, they will not buy anything from you. Individuals usually buy from the ones they trust. So, build that trust with an effective marketing strategy and then approach them.

Chapter 16

The Importance And Role Of
A Self-Publishing Mentor

One of the most helpful ways to improve your self-publishing business is by getting guidance from a skilled mentor. Publishing a book on your own is quite challenging, especially if you are new to this whole procedure. You need to go through so many processes, have to make many choices, and you may even need to keep up with the funds available to you at that moment. This can all get complicated if you are the sole person thinking and working on your project.

However, when you choose a self-publishing mentor, who has already been through this situation, you are planning a platform for your success in the book industry. A mentor has the experience that he/she has accumulated over years for dealing with publishing books in this field. With his/her help, you can be taken down the right path for building your brand and image among your followers. Plus, it is even possible that you gain more contacts through your hired mentor's help.

Qualities To Look For In Your Hired Self- Published Mentor

A capable mentor will be someone who is ready to counsel and advice you about your work. Such a teacher will be ready to support you directly in your work, giving you tips and tricks to improve the quality of your books. Plus, he/she will also help with the right way of promoting books to make them available for your potential readers as soon as possible.

Mind that a good mentor is not someone who will spoon-feed you in your journey. He/she will be the one who is ready to offer you help if you are ready to help yourself. This strategy is important so that you can become independent at a later stage without relying on someone else to expand your business.

That is what mentors are for. They guide you at every step without completely poking their nose in your work. You are free to decide what is best for you by consulting them on the way. This way, you are learning through your own decisions as you grow your business.

What To Look For In A Self-Publishing Mentor?

Building your self-publishing career is not easy. In fact, managing goals, working on daily chores, socializing, facing unexpected situations, and maintaining your health while focusing on your writing work is not everybody's cup of tea. You need a lot of strength, strategy, and dedication to manage it all flawlessly. That is where a mentor steps in to make you feel motivated and confident at dealing with your work and life at the same time.

But, how are you supposed to find a capable mentor to help you with your self-publishing project? Here are the traits that you need to look for in them:

Your mentor needs to be willing to dedicate himself to guiding you through your self-publishing business. Such a person needs to be a professional in the field, which links you to your personal goals as well as your business goals. So, your primary aspect should be to find someone who will connect with you at a fundamental level to lead you towards more opportunities in your career.

You will always face challenges and hurdles in your life, but a capable mentor will help you avoid them by showing you the right way of building a strategy. He/she will advise you by creating realistic schedules so that you proactively work upon them and achieve results.

• *Your Mentor Needs to Be Bold*

A proficient self-publishing mentor should have the power to mold you into the most productive shape. He or she needs to have faith in you and your abilities for achieving success. Plus, he or she should be able to push you out of your bubble of comfort as much as possible. His or her purpose should be to motivate you when you are depressed or facing writer's block.

With the help of a great mentor, you will not be making excuses or cutting corners as such a mentor will not let you take shortcuts. In addition, you will have to be willing enough to take up the challenge yourself as well. When you are unable to see clearly through your journey as an author, he or she will guide you to witness the bigger picture to help you complete your project.

You should also look for mentors who are ready to share their knowledge in this field completely. After all, you are investing your time and money in them, so you deserve their time and experience to the fullest. Some mentors have multiple mentees, which can be tough to handle at times. You need to make sure that this is not the case for them so that you can avoid choosing mentors who are not completely honest with you. Even if he or she has multiple students to guide, you can still choose them, if they are committed to you during your time.

• *Your Mentor Should Be Clear and Transparent*

A capable mentor should not have any hidden motives. In the end, you should only owe your mentor a sense of appreciation and gratefulness, and nothing else. You both will need to respect each other mutually so that there are no hard feelings in the end. This can only be possible with transparency.

Your relationship with your mentor need not require special favors of any kind that are not related to your main task. Everything that your mentor asks you to do should be purposeful. You should not feel like you are doing something for him or her just to pay your dues. To avoid any confusion later, it is good to have a clear conversation with your potential mentor to learn about what are his or her requirements. You should also get to know how you will be evaluated in your mentorship course for self-publishing. There should also be a written agreement to help keep everything transparent, if needed.

A capable self-published mentor will always support you throughout your business. He or she will not only help you locate your mistakes in business decisions but also celebrate your success in life. He or she doesn't just need to be supportive, but also selfless. He or she should not be jealous of your success. Moreover, he/she should not be egotistical and use you as his/her stepping stone to build his/her own career.

• *Your Chosen Mentor Should Have High Values and Morals*

Finding a mentor that has high integrity will be beneficial to you. If you feel that your preferred mentor does not agree with you on certain subjects, then it may lead to issues for you both, leading to more complications.

It is always advisable to research your potential mentor's background properly to learn about his reputation with other mentees in the past before you hire him/her. Feel free to interview him/her to learn about his or her decision-making tactics so that you have a better approach in the long run.

Mentors with low moral values may be hesitant to discuss or help you with your objectives completely. You do not want such people to be your teachers as it will only lead to mistakes in your business. If you associate with someone who is not respected in this field, then it may be counter-productive for your image as well. Choose someone who is sincere in this business so that you can learn to become successful from him/her.

Searching for an expert who will stay with you throughout your self-publishing career would be your best option. Find someone who will commit himself/herself to guide you and help you climb the ladder of success. You want someone who will be there when you need him or her the most.

• *Your Chosen Mentor Needs to Be Communicative*

Good communication is the one where both parties speak and listen mutually. If your mentor is all about speaking and not about listening, then you will not be able to share your personal issues with him or her. You should choose a mentor who will listen to your doubts and give you suggestions and solutions. Finding someone who just lectures you all the time without listening to you even for a bit will only worsen the situation.

Remember that you do not need a spoon-feeder, but a guide who helps you overcome problems as you progress through your self-publishing business. He or she should help you develop a practical plan to win over your audience and keep churning out great book after book to build a six-figure passive income as soon as possible.

• *Your Mentor Needs to Show Dedication*

Mentoring requires one to invest his or her time for you. If your mentor keeps saying that he or she is busy and will not be able to help you on any particular day, then it will only be bad for you. You will need to choose someone who is dedicated to helping you achieve your goals. When such a person dedicates his precious time for you, then it is significant that you too are giving your full-fledged time to him or her. So, be careful about that.

• *Your Mentor Needs to Show Compassion*

There may be situations where you are not able to complete certain tasks given to you by your mentor. Your chosen teacher should know how to handle such situations without showing aggression or anger. You are already aware of your own mistakes, so you do not need a mentor who keeps criticizing your work to point out your errors. Instead, choose someone who is compassionate towards you and connects with you through a level of emotional intelligence and empathy to motivate you on your worst days. So, choose the one that will not use your lack of skills against your decisions.

• *Your Mentor Needs to Be Patient with You*

You cannot call a person a mentor if he or she is not patient enough to guide you properly. Not everyone has the same level of perception and intelligence. Some require extra help, which is why your mentor should see things eye to eye with you and be patient about it. He or she has to keep track of what you do about assigned tasks every day and note the time you take to do it. That way, he or she will decide where you are lacking, thus guiding you properly to stop repeating any negative activities. But, your part as a mentee is to make sure you respect your mentor's patience towards you.

Where To Find Self-Publishing Mentor?

Plenty of online platforms exist that have mentors available to guide and help you with your projects. You can do internet searches for locating self-published mentors to help you with your niche. In addition, you can even research them by learning from their profiles, pages, and joined communities.

Several mentors who are also public speakers are available to provide their services through their self-made brands. Such professionals dedicate their time and effort for the wellness of their students. Finding them is super easy nowadays thanks to the power of the internet. A single email or phone call can get you connected to them and make your self-publishing business head down the right track to fame and prosperity. All you need to do is choose the right one for your needs.

This will help you figure out how good they are in this business. Potential mentors can then be contacted through email, etc. You can let them know your situation so that they can analyze it for you and give you the required help you need.

If you still have doubts about finding the perfect self-publishing mentor for your business, then you can go through this **mentorship program** to help you with your work.

Conclusion

There is no doubt that a self-publishing business is one of the most successful and independent businesses today. After all, so many brilliant authors, who had not been able to gain popularity before, are now lining up to share their masterpieces with the world. It had been pretty hard before, but technological advancements have cleared the paths for independent authors to reach new levels.

If you are planning to become a successful self-published entrepreneur too, then you ought to learn from professionals who have been in this business for many years. Their experience will guide you to achieve at least a six-figure passive income. However, it all depends on how you choose their mentorship skills for your projects.

Such courses are not based on magical attributes that will make you a successful author overnight. You need patience, hard work, and dedication to master each and every concept taught to you in various self-publishing business courses. All you need is to get your act together and find the right mentor to help you achieve your targets.

Also, keep in mind that your hired mentor will guide you through the process of becoming a successful self-published author. His or her influence will make you stand out amongst other competitors as long as you are willing to put an effort towards it. You will need to pull up your socks to achieve your goals for it.

In addition, you will need help with the best courses available to you so that have the perfect guidance for it right from the start of your career as an author.

To help you, you can go through this **YouTube channel** to learn ways from the experts in this field.

I hope that you were able to learn something new and informative from the above chapters. You may have read some of the information mentioned above through various online platforms, but implementing it in your independent author business may not have been possible, until now. Through the various course links offered to you in each chapter, you will be able to learn about not just surviving but thriving in the world of self-publishing. If you give a couple of hours every day to the courses provided to you in this eBook, you will feel the excitement build inside you with fresh creativity and insights.

All you need is to pull up your socks right now and start off with building a fabulous career in the world of self-publishing.

Hope you had a good read!

References

https://publishdrive.com/self-publishing-costs/

https://www.millcitypress.net/author-learning-center/determine-your-budget

https://qz.com/1240924/are-ebooks-dying-or-thriving-the-answer-is-yes/

http://authorearnings.com/report/january-2018-report-us-online-book-sales-q2-q4-2017/

https://www.thebookdesigner.com/2016/02/importance-of-keywords-to-ranking-your-book-on-amazon/

https://myworkfromhomemoney.com/amazon-categories-keywords-books/

https://www.smithpublicity.com/2016/06/why-a-subtitle-is-so-important-in-book-marketing-and-book-publicity/

https://www.draft2digital.com/blog/the-psychology-of-a-good-book-cover/

http://www.koehlerbooks.com/the-importance-of-cover-design/

https://www.thebookdesigner.com/2011/02/authors-wondering-how-long-your-book-should-be/

https://www.authormedia.com/why-your-book-should-audio-book/

https://www.acx.com/help/how-you-benefit/200485370

https://scribewriting.com/write-book-description/

https://publishdrive.com/amazon-ams-ads-how-to-use-them/

http://www.leveluplifestyle.net/kindle-publishing-what-are-review-swaps/

http://www.leveluplifestyle.net/kindle-publishing-how-to-hire-your-first-kindle-virtual-assistant/

https://www.ingramspark.com/blog/what-you-need-to-know-about-translating-your-book